FOUNDATION OF THE GUYANA DEFENCE FORCE

A SOLDIER OF VALOUR STORY

Compton Hartley Liverpool

Coauthor Khalilah Megan Campbell

authorHOUSE®

AuthorHouse™
1663 Liberty Drive
Bloomington, IN 47403
www.authorhouse.com
Phone: 1 (800) 839-8640

Published by AuthorHouse 05/02/2016

ISBN: 978-1-5246-0578-0 (sc)
ISBN: 978-1-5246-0579-7 (hc)
ISBN: 978-1-5246-0577-3 (e)

Library of Congress Control Number: 2016906911

Print information available on the last page.

Contents

A Special Dedication

To my loving mother Mrs. Christina Thomas-Hall who was born on January 9, 1916 and has attained the age of 100 years old on January 9, 2016. I pray that the Lord continue to bless her with health and strength as she lives from day to day.

Dedication

To Lieutenant Colonel Robert Bernard Stephenson, an influential Officer, who was inspirational and emphatically motivated my determination and passion to succeed in my career.

To the military brilliance and leadership of a number of Officers and ranks who I have had the privilege to serve with in my thirty-five year military career in The British Guiana Volunteer Force, The Guyana Defence Force and the Guyana National Service.

To Officers and ranks for their courage and commitment in the Defence of Guyana at Eterinbang (October 1966 and January 1970), the Rupununi Uprising (January 1969), and at Camp Jaguar in the New River Triangle, and the members of the Reconnaissance Platoon who were aboard the first aircraft that landed and took the airstrip at Camp Jaguar on August 19th 1969.

To all members of the Guyana Defence Force (GDF) past, present, and especially, future, to them this book is dedicated.

Acknowledgement

I acknowledge, with infinite and sincere gratitude, the contributions of Horace M. Smith and Clairmonte A. Griffith whose persevering dedication, enthusiasm and encouragement was vital to my effort in transforming my stories perspicuously, on a comprehensive spectrum for sustainable significance and especially Reverend Calvin Clarke and Maxwell Hinds.

Foreword

The following pages of this manuscript recount the researched developmental history, my personal experiences, and memoirs as a participating member of the Guyana Defence Force.

British Guiana had been a colony of the British Commonwealth of Nations for over 200 years. However, for 100 years preceding the British conquest, it had experienced waves of colonization by the European powers of France, Holland and eventually Great Britain respectively. As was customary during the European expansionist strategy of the 'New World', repressive forms of policing control (enslavement, constabulary, and military) were enacted upon a captured and mostly enslaved population.

This period of European domination of the Western Hemisphere began in the late 15th Century and continued for more than a hundred years after the 1838 Abolition of Slavery in British colonies.

In the second half of the 20th Century, a gradual transition from British rule to territorial national independence began for the English-speaking colonies of the British Caribbean. These new sovereign colonies would subsequently become responsible for their own enforcement of order and administration of justice.

British Guiana (South America), along with British Honduras (Central America), Jamaica, Trinidad & Tobago, Barbados, and other English-speaking Caribbean islands were politically regarded as British Caribbean nations. In 1962, Britain granted independence to the first Caribbean territory, with British Guiana gaining its independence in 1966. Thereafter, British Guiana changed its name to Guyana.

The primary focus of this book is on the Guyana Defence Force - its formation, development, operations, service and execution of duties. Since both government and society impact the functioning of such a law enforcement unit, this book records and highlights relevant socio-political events, but only to provide pertinent chronological context.

It is not a commentary on political issues.

HE CAME UP THROUGH THE RANKS

Chapter 1

The United States Military in British Guiana – 1941

On September 3rd, 1939 the Second World War begun with hostilities declared between Germany on the one hand, and Great Britain and her Commonwealth, along with her European allies France, Belgium, Holland and Poland, on the other. At that time they were five Militia Companies in the colony of British Guiana. The five Companies were consolidated into three regular Companies that became part of the South Caribbean Force of the British Army.

On June 3, 1940 Great Britain granted the United States "leases free from all rent and charges for ninety nine years" in various locations of her Colonies including British Guiana, for naval and air bases. This was known as the "Destroyers for Bases Agreement" which was essentially a precursor to the Lend Lease (Disposal of Arms) Act of March 11, 1941, also known as U.S. Public Law 77-11 which provided $50 Billion in Military credits to Britain and its allies which included Russia.

The Destroyers for Bases Agreement was enacted on Sept 2, 1940 in response to Germany's increasing success during the beginning of World War II. The British forces were in desperate need of ships to fight as the German armies moved quickly into France in June 1940.

Further, between November 1939 and June 1940, Britain had sustained the loss of 24 destroyers, 6 (HMS Grafton - Pendant # H-89, Grenade # H86, Wakeful # H88, Basilisk # H11, Havant #H32, Keith) in 4 days (May 29 - June 1) to the German Navy and Airforce (Luftwaffe) which prompted newly elected British Prime Minister Winston Churchill to request help from President Roosevelt. In response, the United States agreed to deliver 50 over aged warships left over from WWI. The destroyers, for Bases Agreement was intended to circumvent the prohibition on involvement in foreign affairs that was required in the Neutralization Act passed by the U.S. Congress in 1935.

American surveyors, engineers and military personnel came to Georgetown, capital of British Guiana, in 1941 and earmarked a site at Hyde Park about twenty-five miles up the Demerara River on its eastern bank. There they started construction of an airbase. The facility they developed still exists and is now known as the Cheddi Jagan International Airport.

The American construction program included:

- A runway that could accommodate long range aircraft. The original runway has been steadily improved over the years and it now accommodates international commercial jets.

- A bomber dispersal circuit (to lessen the impact of air raids or shelling on sitting aircraft, ammunitions and maintenance infrastructure) for their B17 (Flying Fortress) bombers and Dakota transport craft. This is now known as the South Dakota Circuit where motor racing is held.

- A wharf for ocean-going vessels on the Demerara River at the site opposite of what is now the Timehri Police Station.

- A road network that linked various facilities and accommodations. This network also provided access to the East Bank road and the City of Georgetown.

Among the many buildings the Americans constructed that we can still recognize are:

- A hospital complex that is now the Guyana Defence Force Headquarters of Camp Stephenson.

- Barrack rooms for their officers and other ranks which are now the Guyana Defence Force Officers and Sergeants Messes.

- The married quarters that are now the bungalows situated immediately west of Camp Stephenson.

Most of these buildings are still standing today. Other facilities still recognizable today even if their purpose has become redundant or has been abandoned are a power station, a water filtration plant, a swimming pool (first in the Nation), and an ice making plant.

The American soldiers also established a horticultural farm that supplied them with all their green vegetables, and a large chicken farm that reduced the importation of frozen meat. The Base at Hyde Park was named Atkinson Field, after their Commanding Officer Major Atkinson.

On June 20, 1941, Atkinson Field opened, with a mailing address of: U.S. Army Postal Service, A.P.O. 857 Atkinson Field, Georgetown, British Guiana

In October 1941, the 44th Reconnaissance Squadron (Medium Range) under the command of Brigadier General Richard T. King arrived at Atkinson Base from Howard Field, Canal Zone (CZ), Panama.

The task of the 44th Squadron was to perform over water reconnaissance to intercept and destroy hostile naval forces. They also flew antisubmarine patrols.

The Air Echelon consisted of 15 officers, 39 enlisted men, one B-17 and five -18's; subsequently followed by A28's and A 29's (Light Bombers).

The Ground Echelon consisted of three officers, one cadet, and 165 enlisted men who arrived on November 4, 1941 aboard the United States Army Transport ship (USAT) "Franklin S. Leisenring."

U.S. bomb groups were classified into four types:

Very Heavy (VH), Heavy (H),

Medium (M) and Light (L).

Very Heavy = B -29 Super Fortress, B 32 Dominator. Heavy = B -17 Flying Fortress, B - 24 Liberator.

Medium = B-18 Bolo, B-25 Mitchell, B-26 Marauder. Light = A-20 Havoc, A-26 Invader (both types were also attack aircrafts), and A 28/A29.

The U.S. bases in the region were of *vital importance* as they passed thousands of aircraft to the south of Europe, Africa, Middle East, India, China, Burma and elsewhere.

Most of the southern route lay over two great land masses, the South American and African continents. Through the Caribbean the Antilles chain formed convenient steppingstones from Southern U.S. States (Florida) to the Guianas. For a time the Atlantic, approximately 2,000 miles at the narrowest presented a formidable barrier to the movement of two and four engine aircrafts from continent to continent as they lacked the flying range. The air range of the bombers were less than 2,000 miles / 3,219 km thus incapable in crossing the Atlantic Ocean from any base located in mainland USA, consequently a "Southern Air Route" was established and the route from South Florida with distance, are as follows:

Homestead Air Base, South Florida to:

Borinquen Field on the western tip of Puerto Rico = 1,015miles / 1,634km.

Coolidge Field, Antigua = 1,325m / 2,132 km

Carlsen Field, Western, Trinidad = 1,650m / 2,655km

Waller Field, North Eastern, Trinidad = 1,630 m /2,623

Atkinson Field, British Guiana now Guyana = 2,018m / 3248km

Paramirim Field, Natal, Brazil = 3,725m / 5,994km

Ibura Field, Recife, Brazil = 3,840m / 6,180 Km

Wideawake Airfield, Ansension Island, South Atlantic Ocean

Wideawake was a U.S. installation located approximately 1,400m /2,260 km from the coast of Brazil, and 1050m /1690 km from the coast of Africa.

(The distance between Atkinson Field and Natal, Brazil is 1,932 miles / 3,108km; Recife, Brazil 2,020 miles / 3,250 km; Ascension Island 3,201 miles / 5150km).

The Allied forces also had access to bases off the coast of West Africa that included: Roberts Field, Liberia; Sierra Leone; Gambia; with additional bases in Ghana; Nigeria (Kano and Maiduguri); Khartoum, Sudan which shares a border with Egypt and Libya.

The Southern Air Route supported the following operations:

Operation Lightfoot: The British offensive in North Africa - 2nd Battle of El Alamein, Egypt.

Operation Torch: The first US Army offensive of the War led by General Patton in North Africa

Operation Husky: The Allied Invasion of Sicily

Operation Avalanche: The Allied Invasion of Italy

It should be noted, the Caribbean was strategically significant because of Venezuelan oil fields and the Panama Canal. The Caribbean held additional strategic significance to the United States. Bauxite was the preferred ore for aluminium, and one of the few strategic raw materials not available within the continental United States. United States military aircraft production depended upon bauxite imported from the Guianas along shipping routes paralleling the Lesser Antilles. The United States defended the routes with over 189 bombers and 202 fighters, and submarines.

In addition, the American aircrafts brought back casualties from the North African campaign to the hospital at Atkinson Field which was listed as the 353rd Station Hospital.

Moreover, as part of the lend-lease agreement with Britain, the American military also built a small Naval Air Station at Makouria to support the operations of a patrol squadron of seaplanes for their anti-submarine missions. Makouria, situated about twenty miles up the Essequibo River, at a point where the river provided a sufficiently long and unobstructed landing area. Construction began in April 1941 and was completed during the fall of 1942.

Chapter 2

Guianese in the South Caribbean Force

As a spin-off of all these war activities, Atkinson Field and to a lesser extent Makouria, quickly became a source of lucrative employment for Guyanese. As a boy growing up in Georgetown during the war, I remembered seeing American soldiers patrolling the streets of Georgetown in their jeeps. Their sub-machine guns were always in view, and those patrols were always two-man patrols. On certain nights the air-raid siren would sound off in Georgetown. Street lights and houses that had electricity would automatically be turned off. I remembered American soldiers rushing into our home, and those similar to the one I lived in. They would blow out the kerosene lamps that we used at night, warning our parents that all lights should be extinguished every time the siren sounded.

In late 1944, the Guianese Companies of the South Caribbean Force left for the war zone in the Mediterranean. Our troops were largely occupied in guarding German and Italian prisoners of war in Sicily and Egypt. Additionally, numerous educated Guianese young people, both male and female, had made their way individually since the commencement of hostilities, to recruiting centres in England and Canada to join up in support

7

of the war. Along with others from all over the British Colonies, they served in every branch of the British Armed Forces and the Merchant Marines.

The Second World War ended in 1945 with the occupation and capitulation of Germany on May 8, and the subsequent unconditional surrender of Japan on August 15, 1945 (formally signed on September 2, 1945) after the nuclear bombing by a Heavy Bomber (B-29) of the United States Army Air Force (USAAF) of Hiroshima on August 6, 1945 and Nagasaki on August 9, 1945.

Guianese soldiers also returned home that year. I remember running down Robb Street to the waterfront, when I heard that the ship carrying the soldiers had entered the harbour. That troopship anchored midstream, and the soldiers whistled and called out to relatives and friends who gathered on Sandbach Parker wharf to welcome them home. The troops disembarked the following day and, led by the Militia Band, paraded down Robb Street into Camp Street to their barracks at Eve Leary. They were demobilized a month later.

Formation of the British Guiana Volunteer Force (BGVF)

In 1948 the British Guiana Volunteer Force (BGVF) was formed. The core members of this new unit came from among the soldiers who had returned from the war. They became the senior Commissioned Officers and the Warrant Officers, who would lead the 600 member part-time force. The establishment of the British Guiana Volunteer Force comprised of a Battalion Headquarters, a Headquarters Company and five Rifle Companies. A, C and D Companies were based in Georgetown, B Company in New Amsterdam, Berbice and E Company at Mackenzie the bauxite mining town up the Demerara River.

8

The role of the British Guiana Volunteer Force was mainly ceremonial; holding parades on such occasions as the Monarch's Birthday, Empire Day, and Remembrance Day; and also providing the Guard of Honour for visiting Royalty and other dignitaries from associated territories. The secondary role of the British Guiana Volunteer Force was to aid the civil powers in times of crisis. Originally, the Commissioner of Police was head of the BGVF, with the rank of Colonel and the appointment of Commander of Local Forces. Battalion Commanders were all Lieutenant Colonels; among those were Robert Bernard Haywood, Toby Bernard, and CelsoDe Freitas.

Lieutenant Colonel Robert Bernard Haywood.

The BGVF maintained a permanent staff of sixteen members, led by a Major who was also the Adjutant of the Force. There were five Warrant Officers, six Sergeants and four Corporals. Attached to the Volunteer Force was the British Guiana Militia Band.

In 1950, the United States Government handed over the Atkinson Field base and the naval base at Makouria to the British Guiana Government prior to leaving the country. That same year the Volunteer Force held its first camp at Atkinson Field. In 1951, a Volunteer Force construction unit travelled to Tacama located in the Intermediate Savannahs one hundred miles up the Berbice River. There, they rebuilt a defunct military camp which was renamed Camp Haywood in honour of their first Commanding Officer. That same year, Her Royal Highness Princess Alice, Countess of Athlone, a cousin of the British Monarch, presented Regimental Colours to the British Guiana Volunteer Force.

Constitution Conflict

In 1953, a political party, the Peoples Progressive Party led by Dr. Cheddie Jagan and his wife Janet Jagan, Linden Forbes Sampson Burnham, Sydney King, Jainarine Singh, Joseph Pariag Latchmansingh, Ashton Chase and Brindley Benn, won a general elections conducted under adult suffrage by defeating the United Democratic Party led by John Carter. The Peoples Progressive Party formed a new government but on a daily basis the three newspapers the Daily Chronicle, Daily Argosy, and Guiana Graphic, would accuse the government of being communist and the Jagans of being actual members of an international communist alliance. As a consequence, Great Britain fearing a communist take-over of its South American Colony, and a setback in the emerging "Cold War" with the Soviet Block, deployed a battalion of the Welch Fusiliers to British Guiana.

The 1st Battalion, Royal Welsh Fusiliers arrived from its British West Indies base at Up Park Camp, Jamaica, and from British Honduras aboard two frigates, HMS Bigbury Bay and HMS Burghead Bay each carrying 100 men and 10 tons of supplies, and the cruiser HMS Superb with 500 men on board. After two weeks in the country, the regiment was replaced in October 1953 by 1st Battalion Argyll and Sutherland Highlanders. The troops disembarked at Atkinson Field Wharf on the East Bank Demerara River. Upon their arrival, some soldiers were transported by truck to New Amsterdam in Berbice, and based at the BGVF Drill Hall in the Police Station Compound, at New Amsterdam, Berbice. The other soldiers were transported from Atkinson Field Airport, to their Barracks at the former United States of America, Air Force Base, situated at Atkinson Field, East Bank Demerara. They were immediately stationed at these locations, on standby, for any eventual disturbances.

Ultimately, the Governor of British Guiana Sir Alfred Savage embodied the British Guiana Volunteer Force, to perform key point duties at the Kingston Power Plant, Georgetown, the Ramsburg Bulk Fuel Installation at Providence on the East Bank Demerara, the Demerara Radio Station, Georgetown, the Transmitting Station at Sparendaam East Coast Demerara, and the Georgetown Water Works on Vlissengen Road. The British Government then suspended the constitution of British Guiana and dismissed the Peoples Progressive Party Government.

HE The Governor inspecting the BG Volunteers.

During that same week, British Air Force Canberra aircraft flew over Georgetown for the first time with bomb doors open as an exhibition of military power. The Governor, Sir Alfred Savage then appointed an Interim Government of twenty-four non-elected citizens to the House of Parliament. Further, The Interim Government commenced their responsibilities of governing British Guiana from October 1953 to 1957.

After the suspension of the British Guiana constitution, members of the Peoples Progressive Party (PPP) were banned from visiting the Corentyne Coast. Dr. Cheddie Jagan, Brindley Benn, and Neville Anibourne disobeyed the ban. As a consequence, they were arrested and charged. At trial, they were each convicted and sentenced to one year in jail. A building near Atkinson Field Airport was converted into a prison for these three convicted members of the PPP; where, they were imprisoned, for the duration of their sentences. The prison was guarded by members of the British Guiana Volunteer Force, under the command of Captain Clarence Price.

In 1954, the British Guiana Government constructed additional accommodations for the British troops at Eve Leary at the corner of Young Street and Camp Road. The facility was named the Balaclava Barracks. British troops resided at these barracks until they departed from Guyana in October 1966. This former barracks is now the Guyana Police Force Training School.

In January 1956, I joined the BGVF in response to an advertisement for recruits in the Daily Chronicle. I was interviewed, and selected on the same day to be a member of the BGVF, in an intake, that consisted of one hundred new recruits. Among my squad mates, were Ulric Pilgrim, Norman McLean, Randolph Chase, Eugene Tulloch, and Mortimer Niles. This Recruits' Course commenced in January 1956 and concluded in July of the same year.

Ninety recruits were posted to C Company; twelve of us including me were appointed to the rank of Lance Corporal.

Our Company Commander was Major David Jones, the Second in Command was Captain Cecil Martindale, the Company Sergeant-Major was Warrant Officer William Duncan, and there were three Platoon Sergeants, Romahlo, Sumner and Cummings. The Lance Corporals, all of whom received their promotion after successfully completing recruit training, became Section Commanders. There were no Platoon Commanders.

The Company travelled to Tacama Battle School located 100 miles up the Berbice River, in the Ituni Savannahs, in August of the same year with the remainder of the Battalion. There were four other Companies accompanying ours to Tacama for training. These Companies were A, B, D, and E. 'A' Company was commanded by Major Lewis Martin, 'B' Company by Major David Shepherd, 'D' Company by Major Owen Green, and 'E' Company by Lieutenant Basil Roberts. We travelled at night by Transport and Harbours boat for approximately twelve hours. We disembarked the riverboat at 0600 hours then trekked for six miles to get to camp, only to find it unoccupied and over grown with grass. As we assembled, we were greeted by biting sand flies.

The companies were allocated to their billets which consisted of five barrack rooms, an Officers Mess, a Sergeants Mess, an Other Ranks Kitchen and Mess Hall, a Guard Room, and outdoor toilet facilities. In the kitchen, the cooking was done on wood-burning stoves. The barrack rooms were approximately 100 feet long, 30 wide and 15 feet high. The foundation of each Barrack room was built on sand and the roof covered with zinc sheets. There were three full walls made of clay bricks, but the clay brick at the front of each Barrack room wall was only 8 feet high. The other seven feet, was covered by tarpaulin, with the option to remain opened or closed as required. However, it was rolled down and covered completely during rainfall and emergencies. There were two entrances at both ends of the Barrack rooms that always remained open.

The Drill Square was in the middle of the Camp, and our bathing facility was at the Tacama Creek that was about 200 yards from the Camp. The Battle School Power Plant supplied the electricity to the Camp. For our water supply, the Camp had a mobile water tank which was wheeled to Tacama Creek every day, to be filled with water and returned to the Camp. Because it was sand and no wooden floors in the Barrack rooms, we slept in hammocks. On a daily basis we would have to kill snakes that had found their way into our quarters.

For breakfast we ate sardines, corned beef, luncheon meat, an occasionally boiled eggs, salted biscuits or bread, and we drank coffee. For lunch and dinner we consumed stew beef and rice every day. Our training commenced at 0800 hours and concluded at 1100 hours. Training consisted of section and platoon battle drills, all conducted during the hot sun and on the burning sand. Being at Tacama was a new experience for most of us. At Tacama, there are many hilly savannahs that are surrounded by jungle, with several creeks running through it. It is so hot during the day that the animal life, mostly deer, jaguars, and foxes only become active after sunset. At night, the Other Ranks Mess Hall was converted into a canteen for the soldiers.

Chapter 3

Re-Organization of the BGVF

In 1957 the Commissioner of Police was no longer head of the Volunteer Force; consequently, he did not retain the rank of Colonel or Commander of Local Forces. However the British Guiana Militia Band was integrated into the Police Force, and was later renamed The British Guiana Police Force Band. Further, in 1957 Corporal Norman McLean of 'C' Company and Corporal Cecil Glasgow of 'A' Company, were commissioned with the rank of Second Lieutenant.

The period of the Interim Government ended in 1957, and general elections were held in November. There was a split in the membership of the Peoples Progressive Party and it was divided into two factions. Contesting the elections were the Jaganite faction of the PPP led by Dr. Cheddie Jagan, the Burnhamite faction of the PPP led by Linden Forbes Sampson Burnham, and the United Democratic Party led by John Carter. The Jaganite faction won the elections and formed the Government with Dr. Cheddie Jagan as Premier.

In May 1958, the entire British Guiana Volunteer Force was embodied in Georgetown for the visit of Her Royal Highness Princess Margaret, the sister of the reigning British Monarch Queen Elizabeth II. Princess Margaret arrived in British Guiana on the Royal Yacht Britannia, and as part of the visit she was to present the Queens Colours to the British Guiana Volunteer Force. A Presentation and Trouping of the Colours ceremony was scheduled to be held on the Eve Leary Parade Ground in Kingston, Georgetown. However, due to heavy rainfall the outdoor ceremony was not possible at that time. As a result, an indoor event was held at the Transport and Harbours Wharf in Water St. Kingston; in the presence of a Guard of Honour, commanded by Major David Jones. Her Royal Highness Princess Margaret presented the Queens Colours to Lieutenant Robert Bernie Stephenson.

The BGVF was again embodied in the month of June for the Trouping of the Colours which took place at Eve Leary Parade Ground in Kingston, Georgetown. The parade was commanded by Lieutenant Colonel Charles Bernard. The Parade Regimental Sargent Major was Warrant Officer 1, Clement Pilgrim. This is the only occasion that a Warrant Officer can carry his sword on Parade. The Colour Party was comprised of 2nd Lt. Lieutenant Norman McLean, who carried the Queens Colours, and Lieutenant Robert B. Stephenson who carried the Regimental Colours. The two escorts for the Colour Party were Staff Sgt. Arthur Ford and Staff Sgt. Edridch Phillips. 'A' Company commanded by Major Lewis Martin, was the Escort for the Colours. The other detachments on the parade were 'B' Company, commanded by Major David Shepard, 'C' Company commanded Major David Jones, and 'D' Company commanded by Captain Barry Nichols. The Governor, Sir Patrick Reninson, took the salute after which the Parade marched pass the Governor in slow and quick time, giving the eyes right on both occasions. The parade then advanced in review order and presented arms; shortly thereafter the ceremony ended.

In October 1958, 2nd Lieutenants Norman McLean and Cecil Glasgow along with Cecil Roberts of the Queens College Cadets were appointed the first Cadet Officers in the British

Guiana Police Force. Also, in 1959, 1960 and 1961, the BGVF continued to attend weekly training parades that were held every Monday, and to mobilize for annual training that was held for two weeks at Tacama Camp. For our attendance at the weekly training parades, we were paid the tidy sum of one shilling per parade. However, when the Volunteer Force was embodied, or we attended the annual training camp at Tacama, we were paid the same salary as the Police Force.

In February 1960, Captain Cecil Martindale was promoted to the rank of Major. He was then appointed Officer Commanding 'C' Company. In the month of August 'C' Company went to Tacama with the rest of the Battalion to participate in the BGVF annual training. The training entailed minor tactics in Section, Platoon, and Company battle drills. These drills were Advanced, Defence, Withdrawal, and Counter Attack. In addition to the drills, there were competitions among the 5 Companies. 'C' Company participated in eight competitions. There was shooting, throwing a hand grenade, bayonet fighting, tug –of –war, volleyball, several athletic events, and the drill competition. We won these seven events, but lost the football competition to 'A' Company. As a result, 'C' Company was declared the Champion Company.

In October 1960, the BGVF was granted the Freedom of the City of Georgetown. The Force received this honour from the Mayor of Georgetown, Sir Lionel Luckhoo. There was a parade led by 'C' Company and Commanded by Major Cecil Martindale to mark the occasion, British Guiana Volunteer Force soldiers marching through the streets of Georgetown with fixed bayonets for the first time.

In 1961, national elections were contested by the Jaganite faction, the Peoples Progressive Party; the Burnhamite faction now renamed the Peoples National Congress, and the United Democratic Party. The PPP won the elections and remained the governing party. However, trouble erupted shortly after over a pay dispute with the civil servants and other government employees.

In 1962, the British Guiana Trade Union Council called a general strike. The only government institution that was not on strike was the British Guiana Police Force. The Governor, Sir Patrick Renison embodied the British Guiana Volunteer Force to perform key point duties at Kingston Electric Power Plant; Ramsburg Bulk Fuel Installation at Providence; the Demerara Radio Station in Georgetown; the Transmitting Station at Sparendaam; and the City of Georgetown Water Works. The BGVF was also ordered to guard the General Post Office, the largest government building in British Guiana. It was reported that many of the civil servants had broken the strike and returned to work. As a result, the building had to be guarded against retaliation from the striking workers.

On Friday, February 16th 1962, there was a disturbance at the Rice Marketing Board. It was rumoured that the police had killed one person. Unruly citizens began running down Water Street looting and setting fire to stores. A police riot unit was deployed in Water Street outside Bookers Universal Store where they confronted the crowd. As a result; it was forced to fire rubber bullets and tear gas grenades into the unruly crowd; which retaliated by hurling bricks and bottles; they even threw back tear smoke grenades at the police forcing to retreat in front of Sandbach Parker stores. The situation on Water Street outside Sandbach Parker Stores remained unresolved until the sound of a bugle signalled the arrival of a platoon of British soldiers from the Royal Hampshire Regiment. The Platoon had signed the necessary authorization documents with the Police Force, before taking over the duties of the Police Force.

They established a line across Water Street with tape. Further, they displayed a banner that stated "Anyone crossing this line will be shot." One man in the crowd picked up the tape, and started to dance with it. As a consequence of his action, he was promptly shot and killed. After that, the crowd quickly dispersed some running up Water Street into Tiger Bay and Kingston, while others ran down Water Street towards South Georgetown and Albouystown. The British soldiers then marched slowly up Water Street, where they encountered looters in Bookers Universal Store. At the store, they shot and killed one of the looters, Mr. Hyder Khan of Princess Street, Wortmanville. After that, they ordered others to lie face down in the store to wait for the police. The police arrived in their Black Mariah vans and immediately began arresting the detained looters.

Another incident that occurred during the same period took place on Robb Street. A crowd had converged outside Freedom House, throwing bricks and bottles because it was rumoured that a small child had been killed. A police riot unit that included Assistant Superintendent of Police James Phoenix, under the command of Superintendent Derrick McLeod, a white expatriate officer, arrived at the corner of Robb and Wellington Streets and confronted the crowd. Shots were fired, and Superintendent Derrick McLeod was shot and later died of his injuries. Assistant Superintendent James Phoenix and four policemen were seriously injured. The Police withdrew with his body to Camp and Robb Streets. A platoon of British soldiers arrived at the corner of Robb and Camp streets, and marched down Robb Street in quick time. This resulted in the crowd eventually dispersing. Superintendent Derrick McLeod was buried in St. Sidwells Church Yard, at the corner of Vlissingen Road and Hadfield Street, Lodge Village. The strike ended eight days later.

New Constitution of British Guiana

In 1963 a Constitutional Conference on British Guiana was held in Great Britain. The outcome awarded British Guiana a new constitution; with elections to be held under proportional representation in 1964. The conference also determined a date for independence, and with that, responsibility for its own defence. Also, in 1963 construction of a military barracks commenced on what was the former Thomas Lands Rifle Range. When the barracks was completed it was named "Thomas Lands Headquarters" and later renamed "Camp Ayanganna."

In 1964, recruitment of a Special Service Unit (SSU) commenced. It was to be the forerunner of a Guyanese Army. The British Guiana Police Force was tasked with the responsibility for administration, discipline, and training of the SSU. The composition of this unit was 50% East Indians and 50% other races. Members of the SSU were called Constables. The Police Force posted many of its Officers and Non-Commissioned Officers (NCOs) to the Special Service Unit. The Government also recruited Raymond Sattaur, a Guianese who was said to have been trained at Sandhurst Officers Cadet School in Great Britain, who lived and worked in Jamaica as an insurance salesman. He was appointed as Commanding Officer of the SSU with the rank of Major. The SSU also recruited six Officer Cadets, Lieutenant Ulric Pilgrim of the BGVF and civilians Carl Morgan, Ramesh Naraine, Desmond Roberts, Asad Ishoof, and Vibert Boodhoo.

In 1964, the British Guiana Agricultural Workers Union called a strike in the sugar industry. This industrial action soon escalated to ethnic hostility between Indian and African Guianese. Consequently, there were disturbances and deadly clashes in Canje Berbice, Mahaicony, the lower East Coast, and the West Coast of Demerara. Many homes were torched and their occupants seriously injured or killed in all these areas. The Police Force was extended from the Corentyne Coast to the West Coast of Demerara. The Governor embodied the BGVF to assist the Police. The BGVF ranks were posted in New Amsterdam and they guarded the Canje Bridge. Other soldiers were posted at all police stations on the East Coast to patrol the lower East Coast. On the West Coast, two companies of

BGVF soldiers under the command of Major Clarence Price and Captain Claude V. Bowen were deployed at Stewartville, this location being in close proximity to Leonora Police Station.

Simultaneously, a Company of British soldiers occupied the senior staff compound of Leonora sugar estate. These soldiers patrolled areas east of Leonora and held periodic road blocks by day and night. BGVF soldiers reported to Leonora Police Station by Sections. Each section comprised of a Corporal and nine men. I was one of those Corporals, reporting to Senior Superintendent Sam Facey, Commander of Operations on the West Coast. He assigned to us the time, place and type of patrol he wanted executed. The BGVF soldiers patrolled Leonora, Uitvlugt including the Casbah, Zeeburg, Zeelugt, and Meten Meerzorg, under Major Cecil Martindale. It also guarded the Peoples Progressive Party (PPP), and the Peoples National Congress (PNC) detainees in Sibley Hall at the Mazaruni Penal Settlement, as well as the ammunition vaults at Ampa on the Essequibo River, and the explosive stores at the stone quarries south of Bartica.

In August 1964, a section of soldiers patrolling Meten Meerzorg, observed arsonists setting fire to a vacant house. As the arsonists ran from the burning building shots were fired and two of them were killed on the public road. When the residents realized that the two arsonists were shot, calm was restored on the West Coast. Additionally, in September 1964, the British Guiana Agriculture Workers Union called off its strike.

In November 1964, general elections were again held in British Guiana. Contesting the elections were the PPP, the PNC and the United Force (UF). The Peoples Progressive Party won the plurality of the seats, but did not have an overall majority. Therefore, a coalition was formed between the Peoples National Congress led by the Linden Forbes Burnham, and the United Force led by Peter D'Aguiar to establish a Coalition Government with the Honourable Linden Forbes Burnham as the Premier.

Overseas Training of Local Officers in the United Kingdom

In January 1965, Officer Cadets Ulric Pilgrim, Carl Morgan, and Ramesh Naraine departed for England, to attend Mons Officer Cadet School, the British Army short term (six months) training facility for new Army Officers. In March 1965, the BGVF held its first Officer Cadet course conducted by Major Michael Hartman of the British Garrison. Some of the Officer Cadets selected to attend, were Malcolm Archer, Eugene Tulloch, Robert Mitchell, Oscar Pollard, Watson Joseph, Keith Dyer, Ramesh Rambarack, and Richard Fraser. In June 1965, 2nd Lieutenants Ulric Pilgrim, Carl Morgan, and Ramesh Naraine returned from their training in England. Officer Cadets Desmond Roberts, Asad Ishoof, and Vibert Boodhoo were already in England attending Mons Officer Cadet School.

In September 1965, the Government decided that the Special Service Unit would be disbanded and a National Army established in its place. Members of the SSU were given the option to stay in the British Guiana Police Force or become members of the National Army. Thirty-five of the SSU decided to join the Army. Of the thirty-five, five were former Police Non-Commissioned Officers (NCO) namely Sgt. Sunny Haniff, and Corporals Frank Davey, Indial Deomangal, Andrew Hartley, and Roy Veerapen. Some of the thirty former Special Service Unit Constables that joined the army were George Angoy, Richard Cummings, Dyal Panday, Roy Khan, Mohamed Khalil, Benny Singh, Leroy Griffith and Victor Wilson.

In October 1965, the BGVF posted twelve of its NCOs to the Army. They were Sergeants Donald Barker, Eric Primo, and Claude McKenzie; and Corporals Alwyn Jordan, Pelham Van Cooten, Ulric Sutton, Roy Dey, Randolph Chase, Ovid Hicks, Maurice Coppin, Mortimer Niles and I. The twelve of us reported to Major Raymond Sattaur at Camp Ayanganna. While there, we were instructed to exchange our uniforms, for new uniforms that were worn by the former SSU. We were also ordered to remove our badges of rank.

On November 1st 1965, the twelve NCOs from the BGVF were sent on a conversion course with the King's (Liverpool & Manchester) Regiment at Atkinson Field. The thirty Constables, who were now called Private Soldiers, from the former SSU, were sent on a separate conversion course with the same Regiment. After three weeks on the course, the two groups were merged as one Platoon under the command of 2nd Lt. Ramesh Naraine. Then, we travelled by train and riverboat to Tacama to be trained by members of the British Parachute Regiment, that was stationed there. The training Officers were Lieutenant Metuchen and Warrant Officer Arnold, called "Rough Jack".

During this period, 2nd Lieutenants Desmond Roberts, Asad Ishoof, and Vibert Boodhoo returned from England. The BGVF Officer Cadet Course had concluded and six Officer Cadets were commissioned to the rank of 2nd Lieutenant. They were Robert Mitchell, Oscar Pollard, Watson Joseph, Keith Dyer, Ramesh Rambarack, and Richard Fraser.

Meanwhile at Tacama, we were being trained in jungle operations for the first time. Section and Platoon battle drills, with live ammunition were also conducted for the first time. We threw live grenades; we navigated by compass day and night. There was a significant emphasis on physical training. After three weeks, the platoon returned to Georgetown for a passing out parade at Camp Ayanganna. The passing out parade was held the following day. The Platoon Commander was 2nd Lt. Ramesh Naraine and Maj. Raymond Sattaur took the salute. Some of the Private soldiers from the former SSU were promoted to the rank of Lance Corporal, and two of them Dyal Panday and Richard Cummings were promoted to the rank of Corporal.

Twelve Non-Commissioned Officers from the BGVF were posted to the Army. However, Sgt. Donald Barker was sent back to the BGVF. Sgts. Eric Primo and Claude McKenzie retained their ranks along with seven Corporals. Cpl. Randolph Chase was reduced to the rank of Lance Corporal, and I was promoted to the rank of Sergeant, for the reason, that I graduated as the top student of the conversion course. I was then appointed Platoon Sergeant for the first recruit Platoon that was posted to the National Army. These recruits were trained by the Middlesex Regiment of the British Army. The Platoon Commander was 2nd Lt. Carl Morgan.

Members of the BGVF who were not yet posted to the Army were being trained by other members of the Middlesex Regiment at the BGVF Eve Leary Headquarters. The soldiers were formed into three Platoons and sent to Camp Ayanganna. The first Platoon departed from Camp Ayanganna for Tacama under the command of 2nd Lieutenants Desmond Roberts, Asad Ishoof, and Vibert Boodhoo.

In December 1965, Officer Cadets David Granger and Joseph Singh departed for Mons Officer Cadet School in England. Shortly thereafter, Officer Cadets Fairbairn Liverpool and Haydock West left for Sandhurst Military Academy, the prestigious training institution for career British Officers. Subsequently, Officer Cadets Harry Hinds and Michael Leitch would also leave to attend Mons Officer Cadet School.

In January 1966, members of the British Army, who were seconded to oversee the establishment of the New Army, began to arrive in British Guiana. They were Lt. Col. Ronald J. Pope, Majors Peter Hitchcock, Anthony Milford Slade, Benjamin Dunkey, Daniel Bevington, Neil Pullen, and Michael Hartland, along with Warrant Officer 1 Ronald Sergeant, and Warrant Officers 2 George Darr, Peter Saville, and Sandy Duffus. Arriving later, were Signal Sgt. Ronald Cameron who trained the Signal Platoon; Warrant Officer 1 Willian Gallagher, Sgt. William Oliver and Catering Sgt. Peter Horse who took charge of Messing Corps.

In mid-January the same year, other Senior Officers of the BGVF were posted to the New Army. They were Majors Clarence Price and Cecil Martindale, Captains Renny Caleb, Vernon Williams, Leonard B. Muss, Robert Stephenson, and Claude V. Bowen. In addition, Majors Clarence Price and Cecil Martindale were primarily involved in documenting the incoming recruits. They were assisted by Cpl. Gerald MacDonald, who was seconded from the British Guiana Police Force. The Medical Officer was honorary Major Dr. Mook-Sang. Simultaneously, two recruit intakes of soldiers began training with instructors of the Training Wing in Camp Ayanganna. These recruits after their training were assigned Regimental numbers 1100 through 1200.

On February 4th 1966, Her Majesty Queen Elizabeth II, Sovereign of the British Empire, accompanied by her husband Prince Philip, Duke of Edinburgh arrived in Georgetown Harbour aboard the Royal Yatch Brittania for a two day visit. Her Majesty came ashore for the first time on British Guiana soil at Sprostons Wharf where she was welcomed by the local dignitaries and a Guard of Honour drawn up from members of the newly forming army. The Guard wore scarlet berets, khaki shirts and trousers (# 2dress) with white belts and rifle slings. Maj. Raymond Sattaur was Commander of the Guard with Lt. Ulric Pilgrim the Ensign. Maj. Sattaur invited the Queen to inspect the Guard and accompanied her through the drawn up ranks, followed by Col. Ronald Pope and her Equerry.

On March 1st. 1966, the first Battalion on the Army was established under Commander Lt. Col. Ronald J. Pope. There were three Rifle Companies, each Company had two Platoons. The first Company, 'A' Company whose Commander was Maj. Neil Pullen. The Platoon Commanders were 2nd Lt. Desmond Roberts of 1 Platoon, and 2nd Lt. Ramesh Naraine of 2 Platoon, and the Sergeants were Sgt. Eric Primo of 1 Platoon, Sgt. Claude McKenzie of 2 Platoon. The Company Sergeant-Major (CSM) was Warrant Officer 2 George Darr.

The second Company, 'B' Company was under the command of Major Peter Hitchcock. Platoon Commanders were 2nd Lt. Asad Ishoof, 1 Platoon, and 2nd Lt. Oscar Pollard, 2 Platoon. Platoon Sergeants were Sgt. Richard Cummings 1 Platoon, and I was Platoon Sergeant for 2 Platoon. The Company Sargent Major was Warrant Officer 2 Peter Saville.

The third Company, 'C' Company under the command of Maj. Milford Slade. There were no Platoon Commanders. Platoon Sergeants were Sgt. Henry Blackette and Sgt. Ovid Hicks. The Company Sergeant Major was Warrant Officer 2 Sandy Duffus.

Later in the year former BGVF officers Captains Leonard B. Muss, Robert B. Stephenson and Claude V. Bowen would join the 1st Battalion as Second in Command of the three rifle companies.

Warrant Officer 1 Ronald Sergeant, was appointed Regimental Sergeant-Major (RSM); Maj. Benjamin Dunkey was appointed Base Commander, at Atkinson Field. Maj. Daniel Bevington was Quartermaster; Maj. Michael Hartland was posted to the Battalion Headquarters; Maj. Raymond Sattaur was appointed Adjutant; Lt. Ulric Pilgrim was appointed General Staff Officer 2; Lt. Carl Morgan was appointed General Staff Officer 3; Warrant Office 1 William Gallagher and Sgt. William Oliver were posted to the Training Wing. Capt. Renny Caleb was appointed Paymaster, and Capt. Vernon Williams was posted to Battalion Headquarters. The Army and the Middlesex Regiment were engaged in a number of joint training exercises, during the period of March until May 25th, 1966.

On May 22, the same year, the BGVF laid up its Colours during a ceremony at St. George's Cathedral in Georgetown. As part of the ceremony, Capt. Claude Bowen carried the Queen's Colours, and 2nd Lt. Richard Fraser, carried the Regimental Colours. Thereafter, 2nd Lt. Frazer handed over The Colours to Lt. Colonel Celso De Freitas the Commanding Officer BGVF. Then Lt. Colonel Celso De Freitas presented The Colours to the Archbishop of The West Indies, Sir Alan John Knight. After accepting the Colours, the Archbishop laid up the Colours in St. George's Cathedral.

Capt. Claude V. Bowen, Sgt. Maj. Arthur Ford, 2nd Lt. Richard Fraser handing over Regimental Colours to Lt. Colonel Celso DeFreitas. (Sgt. in rear unidentified).

St. Georges Cathedral at 143 feet / 43.59 metres high, and is described as "the largest wooden church building in the world".

Chapter 4

Guyana Independence

On May 24th 1966, Prince Edward the Duke of Kent arrived in British Guiana, for its independence celebrations.

Prince Edward The Duke of Kent, 2Lt. Vibart Boodhoo and Capt. Vernon Williams (with sword drawn).

Sgt. Compton Hartley Liverpool standing at ease on the flank with his Lee Enfield Mark 4 Rifle

On May 19th 1966, an expedition to climb to the summit of Mount Ayanganna, in the Pakaraima Mountain Range was led by Guyanese Mountaineer Adrian Thompson. The other members of the expedition were Fred Bowman a private citizen, and five members of the Guyana Defence Force; led by 2nd Lt. Asad Ishoof, with Privates Dennis Stewart, Henry Clenkien, Donald Walters, and Winston Martindale. The expedition left Atkinson Field Airport by a Dakota Aircraft. They landed at the Amerindian (now known as – Indigenous) Village of Imbaimadai airstrip, on the Upper Mazaruni River. From

Imbaimadai they travelled down the Mazaruni River by boat to Chi-Chi Falls (The Mazaruni River is a tributary of the Essequibo River). They departed Chi-Chi falls by foot, and trekked to the Amerindian (N.K.A. – Indigenous) Mission at Chinawying. While at Chinawying, they met their guide to Mount Ayanganna Mr. Isaac Gerry of Phillipai Village. Thereafter, they continued their journey, to the base of Mount Ayanganna. The expedition with the exception of their guide, Mr. Isaac Gerry, reached their destination after travelling for seven days from Georgetown.

On the morning of May 25th, the expedition began their ascent of Mount Ayanganna, which is 6,700 feet high reached the summit by 2200 hours; then they erected a portable flag pole. At 2359 hours, 2nd Lt. Asad Ishoof raised the Flag of Guyana the Golden Arrowhead, as British Guiana became the Independent Nation Guyana on May 26th 1966. After hoisting the flag, they placed a commemorative plaque with the eight names of all the members of the expedition.

L to R: Pvt. Winston 'Bunny' Martindale, Isaac Gerry (Guide), Lt. Asad Ishoof, Fred Bowman, Prime Minister LFS Burnham, Adrian Thompson, Pvt. Henry Clenkien, Pvt. Dennis Stewart, Pvt. Donald Walters.

Synchronously, on the night of May 25th 1966, a Guard of Honour, commanded by Capt. Robert B. Stephenson with a Company of soldiers marched onto the National Park tarmac for British Guiana's Independence Day Ceremony. At 2358 hours, 2nd Lt. Jon Klaas of the Middlesex Regiment lowered the Union Jack. As the Union Jack was lowered, 2nd Lt. Desmond Roberts of the National Army raised Guyana's National Flag, the Golden Arrowhead, for the first time in Guyana. During the Flag-raising, the Military Contingent; gave the "Presentation of Arms." Simultaneously, the National Anthem, "Dear land of Guyana, of Rivers and Plains" was sung for the first time. At that moment in time, British Guiana became the Independent Nation of Guyana.

Parade led by 2LT. Desmond Roberts. Maj. Cecil Martindale standing on lawn

Accordingly, The Premier, Honourable Linden Forbes Sampson Burnham, became the first Prime Minister of Guyana. In his address to the Nation, the Prime Minister named the National Army, the Guyana Defence Force (GDF). With the coming into being, of the Guyana Defence Force, the Ordinance that governed the BGVF expired; thus ending its existence.

At 0900 hours, on that same day, the GDF held its first Guard of Honour at Parliament Building for the opening of Parliament. The Duke of Kent presented the credentials for Guyana's Independence to the Prime Minister Linden Forbes Sampson Burnham. Henceforward, Guyana officially became an Independent Nation.

On June 3rd 1966, 2nd Lieutenants David Granger and Joseph Singh returned from Mons Officer Cadet School. Upon their return, they were appointed Platoon Commanders of 'C'

Company. There were some minor changes in the Guyana Defence Force at that time. As a consequence, Maj. Neil Pullen was posted to the Training Wing, and Maj. Michael Hartland was appointed Officer Commanding 'A' Company, and also, 2nd Lt. Keith Dyer took command of 2 Platoon 'B' Company from Oscar Pollard was posted to the Training Wing.

On June 5th, 1966, The Guyana Defence Force established three locations; that were essentially the billets for the Rifle Companies. They were as follows:

- Camp Ayanganna at Thomas Lands, Georgetown.
- Atkinson Field Base at Atkinson Field, East Bank Demerara.
- The Senior Staff Quarters at Rose Hall Estate, Canje, Berbice.

The three Companies would rotate every six weeks between the three locations. The Company that was based at Rose Hall Estate on its rotation change over, was required to march the distance of seventy five (75) miles from their location to get to Thomas Lands now Camp Ayanganna in Georgetown.

The Company that was at Atkinson Field Base was required to send a Platoon by riverboat RH Carr to Mackenzie for two weeks on familiarization training. On completion of this training, the platoon had to run and walk to return to Atkinson Field Base. The distance from Mackenzie to Atkinson Field Base is forty (40) miles. In those days there was no Linden/Soesdyke Highway, just a trail through the jungle that could accommodate small four wheel drive vehicles.

On this trail, the first Platoon to attempt the Mackenzie/Atkinson Field run and walk exercise was 2 Platoon, 'B' Company led by 2nd Lt. Keith Dyer, and I was the Platoon Sergeant. On the day of the run and walk exercise, we started at 1800 hours and continued through the night. The trail was hilly and sandy with several creeks along the way. The soldiers were energized and committed to finishing the exercise. The entire Platoon completed the run and walk exercise in twelve hours; arriving at Atkinson Field at 0600 hours the next day.

The second Platoon that attempted the same run and walk exercise was 1 Platoon 'A' Company led by 2nd Lt. Desmond Roberts. They were accompanied by Maj. Michael Hartland the Company Commander. It is rumoured that they had to rest for several long periods of time; because their Company Commander Maj. Michael Hartland was an elderly Officer. They finished the run and walk in thirteen and one half hours. Their timing, displeased the Force Commander because he felt the Platoon that was led by a Mons trained Officer, should have beaten the Platoon that was led by a BGVF trained Officer. Since all the other Platoon Commanders were Mons trained, he ordered all of those Platoons to do the run.

In the month of July, Officer Cadets Marcus Munroe and Kennard Ramphal departed to attend Mons Officer Cadet School. Moreover, in 1966, the three Rifle Companies of the GDF held its first training exercise, on the Corentyne Coast at a village called Elogie, located fifteen miles from New Amsterdam. Berbice. While we were there, we dug in defensive position. Facing an enemy from the East, we would withdraw to alternative defensive position. Over a period of one week, one week we reached New Amsterdam, crossed the Berbice River and advanced through the rice fields and coconut walks of Western Berbice. Then we crossed the Abary River, through the rice fields of Burma, and the back lands of Mahaicony. At that point, we carried out an attack at dawn on the Mahaica River and ended the exercise. The Guyana Defence Force also carried out patrols on the East Coast Demerara, and West Coast Berbice. We drew maps of every village highlighting important roads and facilities in the villages.

Venezuela Invades Ankoko Island, Cuyuni River

On October 2nd 1966, Venezuelan troops stationed at Ankoko Island on the Cuyuni River border occupied Guyana's half of the island. This action by Venezuela was in flagrant violation of an International Commission's arbitration and settlement in 1893, of a border dispute between Venezuela and Great Britain. Not only did Venezuela seek to revive its claim to two thirds of Guyana's territory on the spurious and unfounded assertion that the judgement of the 1893 Commission was tainted by fraud, but it also demonstrated that it was prepared to threaten and even use military action in pursuit of its claims to our territory. This hostility by Venezuela towards Guyana has continued unabated from the time of our independence from Great Britain until the time of writing this book in 2015.

A reconnaissance team comprising of the Force Commander Col. Ronald J. Pope, Senior Superintendent of Police Lloyd Barker, and Intelligence Officer Lt. Carl Morgan, flew into Cuyuni by Guyana Airways Corp, Grumman, a twin engine amphibious aircraft that was versatile on water and on land. Upon their arrival they made their way to Eteringbang Village, located opposite Ankoko Island. At Eteringbang Village, there was a long established Police Outpost. The team inspected the Police Outpost because it was the first time that the GDF had they visited the Outpost.

Lt. Carl Morgan at Eteringbang, Cuyuni River Oct 1966

The next day a Dakota (DC-3 / C47) aircraft landed at Kamarang, a village at the confluence Mazaruni and Kamarang Rivers about 50 miles south of Ankoko. On board, was 1 Platoon of 'A' Company led by 2nd Lt. Desmond Roberts accompanied by Company Commander Maj. Michael Hartland. They were transported into the Cuyuni River by Grumman aircraft (sea plane) then occupied a position on high ground adjacent to the Police Outpost at Eteringbang Village. Thus, Guyana Defence Force established its first border location. Later the same day, 2 Platoon "A" Company commanded by Sgt. Claude McKenzie also flew in to Eteringbang. The Army would later occupy locations at Makapa Hills, Ekereku, Kurutuku, Kaikan, Paruima, and Kamarang, all villages along our tension sensitive western border.

On October 10th 1966, the Guyana Defence Force held its first Platoon Sergeants Course at Atkinson Field, where 'B' Company was stationed at the time. Both 2nd Lt. Keith Dyer and I attended the course. It was conducted by Warrant Office 1 William Gallagher and Sgt. William (Bill) Oliver. To commence the training, WO 1 Gallagher instructed us to run the assault course twice a day, once before breakfast and once after lunch. At the completion of the first week, he added a two mile run that started from the fire station at Atkinson Field, and ended at the ice-house. Then we ran through the assault course. WO 1 Gallagher described this as "fun and games" but to us it was otherwise.

In the third week, the Platoon Sergeants Course trainees travelled to Tacama for field training. 'C' Company had previously gone to Base Tacama, for the Force Commander's test exercises. These exercises comprised of several phases: the advance, the defence, the withdrawal to an alternative defensive position, and the counter attack. All aspects of the training were categorized as basic infantry manoeuvers. I was appointed as an umpire on 'C' Company's test exercises that was held for a period of five days. After five weeks, the Platoon Sergeants Course ended in November. Respectively during the same period, I was posted to the Training Wing.

The first changeover of troops occurred at Eteringbang. 2 Platoon 'B' Company led by 2nd Lt. Watson Joseph took over the location from 2nd Lt. Desmond Roberts and his men. Additionally, 2nd Lt. Desmond Roberts and a section of his men were the last to leave Eteringbang by Grumman aircraft. The aircraft ran out of fuel while attempting to land at Kamarang airstrip, and plunged into the jungle a short distance from the airstrip. Fortunately the injuries sustained by 2nd Lt. Desmond Roberts and his men were not serious. They were lucky to escape with just cuts and bruises, but a Guyana Airways dispatcher on the plane broke one of his legs. Due to this accident the aircraft was a totally destroyed.

On December 5th 1966, Col. Ronald J. Pope visited the Sergeant's Mess at Atkinson Field, to meet with the Warrant Officers and Sergeants for the first time. We lined up in the Sergeant's mess hall to be introduced. When he came to me he said *"Sgt. Liverpool, you have far to go in the Guyana Defence Force if you keep up the good work."* On December 15th, the Guyana Defence Force announced its first NCO's promotions. Sgts. Eric Primo, Claude McKenzie, Richard Cummings, Ovid Hicks, Sonny Haniff and Andrew Hartley were promoted to the rank of Staff Sergeant. With their promotions, Cummings, Hicks, Haniff and Hartley were appointed Company Quartermaster Sergeants.

As well, in December, Maj. Peter Hitchcock left the Guyana Defence Force to return to England. Following his departure Capt. Robert B. Stephenson was appointed Company Commander 'B' Company. Maj. Raymond Sattaur also returned to Jamaica. Capt. Ulric Pilgrim was appointed Adjutant. Lt. Desmond Roberts became the new General Staff Officer 2 (G2), and Lt. Keith Dyer was appointed General Staff Officer 3 (G3).

In December 1966, the Guyana Defence Force sustained its first loss of a member, Military Police, Private Jerome Brutus who during rehearsal drills for the ceremonial induction of His Excellency, Sir David Rose as the first Guyanese, and second Governor General (succeeding Sir. Richard Luyt, a British citizen), that died accidentally, from cannon fire while loading the cannon which was mistakenly engaged. He was buried at Le Repentir Cemetry with full Military Honours.

A Land Rover jeep with a limber attached transported the flag-draped casket. One of the most noticeable features of a Military Funeral is the custom of reversing the order of things from what they are normally. When the body is being placed to the place of burial, arms are reversed.

In January 1967 the Reconnaissance Platoon was formed. Lt. Carl Morgan was appointed Platoon Commander, with Sgt. George Angoy the Platoon Sergeant. Some of the best soldiers from the rifle companies became members of this unit. A number of young men from the indigenous villages of St. Cuthbert's Mission on the upper Mahaica River, and from St. Francis Mission on the upper Mahaicony River were directly recruited as scouts, and rather than train as regular recruits, received individual instructions from NCOs within the Platoon. The Reconnaissance Platoon was mobile with a fleet comprised of six Land Rover utility vehicles, four armoured cars, and one three ton truck.

In actuality, all the infantry companies of the 1st Battalion were now fully equipped with their own vehicles, acquired from the departing British Garrison. Each platoon had a troop-carrier

3 ton truck; there were also numerous Land Rovers and other support vehicles available for Commanders, Logistics, Administration and the Signal Communication Unit.

By mid-January 1967, orders were issued by the Government that female soldiers would be allowed into the Guyana Defence Force as Reservists. The Guyana Defence Force high command felt that the Force was not ready for female soldiers, but superior orders prevailed. The Force Commander decided to put together the best possible team to train these female recruits. The team comprised of Maj. Cecil Martindale, Regimental Sergeant Major (RSM) Warrant Officers Class1 Ronald Sergeant, Sergeant William Oliver; Cpl. Mohammed Khalil and me. Cpl. Khalil and I were chosen, because I was the top student on the Platoon Sergeant's course that ended in November, and Cpl. Khalil was the runner-up.

On February 6th 1967, sixty-four female recruits were selected to be trained for the newly formed Women Army Corps, and reported to Atkinson Field to commence training. Four of them were already commissioned as Officers. They were Capt. Joan Granger (elder sister of 2nd Lieutenant David Granger), 2nd Lieutenants Hyacinth King, Brenda Aaron, and Clarissa Hookumchand.

These Officers were to be trained by Maj. Martindale and Regiment Sergeant Major (RSM) Warrant Officers Class1 Ronald Sergeant. The sixty private female recruits were divided into three squads of twenty each. Sgt. Oliver trained the #1 Squad; I trained the # 2 Squad, and Cpl. Khalil trained the # 3 Squad. Training commenced the following day on February 7th 1967, with instructions and practice in foot and arms drill, minor tactics, signals and first aid. The personal weapon issued to each recruits was a Sten sub-machine gun that had a wooden butt.

On the fourth week, the three subalterns were attached to the squads. 2nd Lt. Hyacinth King to #1 Squad; 2nd Lt. Brenda Aaron to

#2Squad, and 2nd Lt. Clarissa Hookumchand to #3Squad. Rehearsal for a passing-out-parade commenced. During the fifth week rehearsal was moved to Camp Ayanganna. On March 15, there was a full dress passing-out-parade at Camp Ayanganna. In attendance was Prime Minister, Lyndon Forbes S. Burnham, members of the Government, and a wide cross section of the Guyanese populace. The parade commander was Capt. Joan Granger and the inspecting officer was Minister of Education Mrs. Winifred Gaskin.

It was a good parade; after the final salute and an address by the Minister of Education Mrs. Winifred Gaskin; it was adjudicated that #2Squad was the best squad on parade. As a result, I was called up to receive a trophy on the squad's behalf. One of my recruits Gwen Davis was also judged to be the best recruit. After a party that same night, the female soldiers were dismissed and sent home the next day.

Instructors, L to R: RSM WO 1 Ronald Sergeant and Sgt. Compton Hartley Liverpool.

In March 1967 a male Reservist Platoon commenced recruit training. Among this intake were Godwin McPherson, Winston Moore, Clairmonte Griffith, and Herbert Moe.

In May 1967, promotions were again announced; Staff Sgts. Eric Primo, Claude McKenzie, and Richard Cummings were promoted to the rank of Warrant Officers Class 2 (WO2) I was promoted from the rank of Sergeant to the rank of Warrant Officer Class 2 (WO2) bypassing the rank of Staff Sergeant.

On May 26 1967, the Guyana Defence Force held its first route march through the City of Georgetown. The parade was led by the Reconnaissance Platoon in their armoured cars, under the command of Lt. Carl B. Morgan. The soldiers, including a detachment of the Women Army Corps, marched through the streets of Georgetown singing "It's Guyana for me and we fight to make you free."

The Song lyrics were composed by Col. Ronald Pope and transcribed into music by Police Superintendent Barney Small, Director of Music of the Guyana Police Force. During that period, the GDF Band was in its infancy. Today, the song is known as "Pope's March" and is included in the repertoire of the GDF band."

Lt. Carl Morgan on top of Armour car presenting a salute to Sir David Rose, Governor General. Also in picture – Col. Pope, GDF Commander, Police Commissioner, Mr. Felix Austin, Senior Supt Dick La Borde (on horseback).

At the end of May 1967, many female Reservists were mobilized for active duty as regular soldiers of the GDF. Some of them became administrative staff, such as typists, clerks in the registry, signallers, switchboard operators, cooks and support staff in the Officers, Sergeants and Other-Ranks Messes, the Ordinance and Ration Stores, and the Medical Centre. One of them was posted to the Guyana Defence Force Band, one to the Intelligence Corps. Also, two of them were appointed to the Military Police, and two as drivers.

In June 1967, Capt. Ulric Pilgrim was appointed Officer Commanding 'C' Company; Capt. Carl Morgan was appointed Adjutant; Lt. Desmond Roberts was appointed General Staff Officer 2, and Capt. Ramesh Naraine, was posted to the Training Wing. In addition, Lt. Joseph Singh was appointed

Reconnaissance Platoon Commander and Lieutenant David Grainger was appointed General Staff Officer 3.

Also in June, Officer Cadets Randolph Johnson, Walter Spooner, and Aubrey Featherstone departed to attend Mons Officer Cadet School.

In July 1967, the Guyana Defence Force held its first athletics sports meeting and Lt. Desmond Roberts was the champion athlete. The Guyana Defence Force also held its first championship NCO competition; Corporal Wilfred Austin of the Reconnaissance Platoon was the champion NCO. For his win, he was presented with a brand new Self-Loading rifle (SLR) by the Force Commander. With this presentation, the weapon was introduced to the army. It replaced the old Lee-Enfield Mark 4 rifle that had been in use since the Second World War. The Guyana Defence Force soldiers had to be trained in the use of the SLR which was a lighter, semi-automatic weapon that carried 20 rounds instead of 5. It was not as accurate as the Lee-Enfield Mark 4.

In August 1967, Privates Godwin McPherson and Winston Moore completed a Trained Soldiers Course. Subsequently, they were then appointed Officer Cadets and posted to Base Camp Ayanganna.

Chapter 5

The Arms Store Robbery

In August 1967, B Company Arms Store was broken into. It was discovered by armourer clerk, Private Stephens that 20 Lee Enfield Mark 4 Rifles and 4 Light Machines Guns were stolen. It was noted, that the thieves made their entry into the arms store, by removing clay blocks from the rear of the arm stores. The arms store was located on the ground level under the base canteen. A large opening was discovered at the northern fence of the Base. It was also discovered, that the robbers made their exit with the arms through the opening. The Battalion Commander, Lieutenant Colonel Ronald James Pope, ordered all the soldiers of B Company to search every square foot of land at Atkinson Field. However, they did not recover any of the stolen arms. The theft occurred during the period when the GDF was converting from the .303 Enfield Mark 4 rifle to the 7.62 mm Self Loading Rifle (SLR).

During a subsequent period, the Reconnaissance Platoon received a tip about where the weapons could be found. They went to the villages of Little and Big Baiabu on the West Bank of the Mahaicony River in search of the weapons. Unfortunately, the weapons were not discovered.

The Battalion Commander, Lieutenant Colonel Pope, then ordered that all the .303 ammunitions that the weapons used, should be withdrawn from the Rifle Companies, and stored in the ammunition dump. He also ordered that the Lee Enfield Mark 4 Rifles, that were issued to the Rifle Companies be withdrawn. Additionally, the Self Loading Rifles (SLR) that used the 7.62 ammunitions to be issued to the Rifle Companies. All the Lee Enfield Mark 4 Rifles, that had been withdrawn, were stripped of its firing bolts and packed in crates. The Lee Enfield Mark 4 Rifles, and all the .303 ammunitions, were loaded onto Transport and Harbours Boat Lady North Court. They were taken and dumped into the Mid-Atlantic Ocean. A new modern arms store was constructed, on the football field at Atkinson Field Base. It was fenced in by 12 feet high barbwire, and was guarded day and night by Sentries.

A Board of Inquiries, convened by the Battalion Commander, Lieutenant Colonel Pope, found that the weapons were stolen by person or persons unknown.

In September 1967, a third platoon was added to each of the three Rifle Companies. I was posted to 'B' Company, and appointed Platoon Commander for 3 Platoon at Base Camp Ayanganna. Keith Dyer and Kennard Ramphal were the other Platoon Commanders. The entire Company went to Tacama to engage in the Force Commander's test exercises.

In the month of October, Officer Cadets Oscar Canzius and Gregory Gaskin left for Mons Officer Cadet School. Likewise in October 1967, Maj. Hartland left the Guyana Defence Force and went to Barbados. As a result, Capt. Leonard B. Muss was appointed Company Commander 'A' Company. On November 1, 1967, Warrant Officer 2 George Darr, left the Guyana Defence Force and returned to England. I was appointed Company Sergeant-Major (CSM) 'A' Company, the first Guyanese Company Sergeant-Major in the Guyana Defence Force, Warrant Officers Eric Primo and Claude McKenzie were appointed

Base Sergeant-Majors at Camp Ayanganna, Georgetown and Atkinson Field respectively.

On November 5, 1967, Senior Police Superintendent Lloyd Barker of the Guyana Police Force, and a detachment of the Tactical Service Unit travelled to Camp Oronoque on the New River in the extreme south-east of Guyana. They found the camp occupied by many Dutch surveyors. The authorities of the Dutch colony of Suriname were trying to establish that what we know as the New River was actually the Corentyne River and thus the true border, because of the greater volume of water compared to what we Guyanese identify as the Upper Corentyne and which they considered a mere tributary.

The Police landed at the location by Grumman aircraft; they called out to the Dutch surveyors who then sent a boat to the aircraft. The Police boarded the boat and went ashore. Once ashore, they took command of the camp, and halted the work of the surveyors. After two weeks, the Dutch Government withdrew the surveyors from that location. Consequently, the police raised the flags of Guyana and the Police Force. They took up position on high ground from which vantage point they could monitor activity on the New River. In November 1967, a Platoon of Guyana Defence Force soldiers, commanded by 2nd Lt. Aubrey Featherstone was sent to Camp Oronoque to support the Police detachment. While there they established a position in the jungle as a temporary base.

In December 1967, 2nd Lt. Fairbairn Liverpool returned after two years at Sandhurst Military Academy. He was later appointed a Platoon Commander in 4 Company. Similarly, in December 1967, Officer Cadets Godwin MacPherson and Winston Moore were commissioned with the rank of 2nd Lieutenants. 2nd Lieutenant MacPherson was appointed a Platoon Commander in 4 Company and 2nd Lieutenant Moore was appointed to Platoon Commander in 5 Company.

On January 2nd 1968, the Second Battalion of the Guyana Defence Force was formed. Lt. Col. Cecil Martindale was appointed Commanding Officer; Capt. Ramesh Naraine was appointed Adjutant; and Warrant Officer William Gallagher was appointed Regimental Sergeant Major. They were stationed at Thomas Lands, Georgetown, now known as Camp Ayanganna. Moreover in January 1968, three rifle companies 4, 5, and 6 were designated to the Second Battalion. Capt. Desmond Roberts was given command of 4 Company; Capt. Carl Morgan was appointed Officer Commanding 5 Company and Lt. Joseph Singh appointed Officer Commanding 6 Company.

Lieutenant Marcus Munroe was appointed Officer Commanding the Reconnaissance Platoon. As Commander, he transformed the highly mobile platoon into one of the finest outfits that operated along the Nation's western borders, where Long Range Reconnaissance Patrols to and between remote Indigenous settlements, helped to showcase the GDF to communities that had little or no contact with the authorities on the coast.

With the coming to being of the Second Battalion, the configuration in the First Battalion changed. Col. Clarence Price was appointed Commanding Officer of the First Battalion and Col. Ronald J. Pope appointed Chief of Staff. Afterwards 'A', 'B' and 'C' Companies were renumbered 1, 2, and 3 Company respectively.

On January 5th, 1968 Officer Cadets Ian Fraser, Franklin Gibbs and Maxwell Hinds departed for England to attend Mons. In the same month 1 Company, Commanded by Leonard B. Muss, was the first Company to be posted to the interior, at Bartica. I was still the Company Sergeant at the time. We travelled by GDF vehicles from Thomas Lands HQ now Camp Ayanganna, Georgetown to the Transport and Harbours Wharf at Stabroek, where we drove our vehicles onto a ferry boat. The boat took us across the Demerara River to Vreed-en-hoop wharf. We drove from Vreed-en-hoop to Parika wharf. From there we took another boat to Bartica wharf, a five hour journey. On our arrival, we disembarked our vehicles then drove to Bartica airstrip. The company went to Bartica to establish a location in the jungle, near the Bartica airstrip.

We assembled in an area in the vicinity of the airstrip; then unloaded our equipment. Our camp-building equipment consisted of power chain saws, axes, cutlasses, machetes, camp cots, mosquito nets, cooking utilities and other survival gear. Once, the equipment was unloaded and secured, we ate our lunch. After lunch, we cut down trees and bushes to clear the land to build the camp. We used the bark from the Baramanni tree to build our accommodations. The Baramanni bark is used for accommodations built for extended stays beyond six weeks and if the location calls for the rotation of troops.

We built accommodations for senior ranks, a mess hall, a kitchen, a pit latrine and a bath facility. The other ranks would sleep in the forest under bush huts called 'Bashas' or 'Swamp Beds' that we also built.

The 'Basha' is a hut for two to four occupants constructed of wooden poles and palm branches obtained from the surrounding jungle, with the floor elevated off the ground to prevent flooding and harmful fauna from disturbing the occupants. For the making of an elevated two-man Basha/ Swamp Bed, the taller of the two soldier's height must be considered before starting. For example, if the taller of the two is 5' 10", the building ofa 6.5 feet long by 5 feet wide structure would suffice.

First, one must identify and mark out the area (6.5' X 5') before commencing.

Secondly, four holes must be dug or driven in the soil approximately 18-24 inches deep at each end of the rectangle with additional holes for uprights for two beds and the elevated floor.

Thirdly, ten straight limbs with forks at one end and sharpened at the other must be cut at three lengths, these poles should be strong enough to support two soldiers and their equipment – four should be knee length, four shoulder length, and two center pieces longer than 6.5 feet which would form the gable (an inverted V that forms two sloping sides) of the hut. Commence placing and securing the fork poles into the dug holes The knee length and shoulder length forks should be placed at each of the four (4) corners with the shoulder ones inserted behind and on the outside of the knee length fork.

Additional poles without forks are required to be cut; two (2) for the 5 feet width, two for the 6.5 foot eves and as many as necessary of equal circumference to cover the 6.5 feet X 5 feet floor, the beds and the rafters. To complete the shelter, cut three (3) limbs/poles longer than 6.5 feet and insert one each into and across the shoulder forks at each end, and one across the center fork. The entire construction is held together with pliable vines.

Upon its completion of the wooden frame, cover the bed frame with leaves or grass to form a sleeping surface. Also place palm branches across the top for shelter. It should be noted that during the rainy season, one's waterproof poncho can be used as additional waterproofing on the roof when not otherwise in use.

The first intake of the Guyana Youth Corps from Georgetown, who were on their way to Tumatumari on the Potaro River, spent one week with 1 Company undergoing training at our camp at Bartica airstrip. After completing the training, they continued on their journey to Tumatumari.

One Company returns to Atkinson Field

After six weeks, 1 Company handed over the Bartica location to 4 Company. Then, 1 Company returned to Atkinson Field. When we were there, we received a telephone call from the Battalion Commander. He asked if we were not submitting any names for the Officer Cadet Training Course at MONS. We submitted three names, Sgt. Victor Wilson, Cpl. Lennox Luncheon and Lance Cpl. George Davidson. Two weeks later it was published in Force Orders that Sgt. Victor Wilson was selected to attend MONS Officer Cadet School.

On January 15, 1968, 1 Platoon commanded by 2nd Lt. Michael Leitch, took over the GDF location at Camp Oronoque on the New River. The platoon commenced militarizing the camp by digging fire trenches and building bunkers, but the Police objected because they felt that the location belonged to them. 2nd Lt. Michael Leitch continued the task until it was completed, then reported the matter to GDF Headquarters at Camp Ayanganna.

As a result, Maj. Leonard Muss Officer Commanding 1 Company was sent to the location with orders to find an alternative site for the Guyana Defence Force outpost. There was a small boat at the location which was owned by a civilian that the Police normally hired. Maj. Muss decided that he would send 2nd Lt. Leitch with the small boat on a reconnaissance of the new position. However, 2nd Lt. Leitch stated that he was apprehensive about taking the small boat, because he could not swim. For that reason Maj. Muss and four soldiers left in the small boat to reconnaissance the location. They reached as far as King Fisher Falls some five miles downriver from Camp Oronoque. At King Fisher Falls, they identified a new location that could accommodate the Platoon. On their way back upriver, the boat engine malfunctioned. As a consequence the boat drifted down the river until they reached a Dutch location. When they arrived there, they were detained by the Dutch Police at a Dutch Camp in New River.

To secure their release there were many diplomatic negotiations by Foreign Minister Shridath Ramphal at The Hague in Holland, since Dutch Guiana was not an independent country as yet. The Hague represented the International Court of Justice, the principal judicial branch of the United Nations (UN).

After they were released, Maj Muss and his men had to pull the boat up river by walking along the bank of the river until they reached a landing pool at Oronoque. Guyana Airways was contacted from Camp Oronoque, to send them transportation. Guyana Airways Grumman aircraft then arrived and transferred the entire Guyana Defence Force Platoon to the new location that was named "King Fisher." The Guyana Police Force was located at Camp Oronoque, and the Guyana Defence Force was located at Camp King Fisher. In April 1968, Maj Ulric Pilgrim and Sgt. Neville White departed for the Far East to attend the British Jungle Warfare School at Johor Bahru in Malaya. Similarly, in April Warrant Officers 2 Claude MacKenzie and Eric Primo went to England to attend the All Arms Drill Course at Pirbright, Surrey, England. In May 1968, Sgt. Victor Wilson and Officer Cadet Keith Ross left for England to attend the Officer Cadet Course at MONS Officer Cadet School.

In May 1968, a section from the Reconnaissance Platoon led Lt. Marcus Munroe, that including Joel Simmons, Bobby Alexander, Errol Bobb, Sahadeo Maraj, Norman Haynes, Gordon Simon, Clairmonte Griffith, and Winston 'Bunny' Martindale (who was making his second trip to the summit) and the guide Isaac Gerry travelled to Ayanganna to replace the flag that was hoisted there on Independence Day May 25-26, 1966.

Ayanganna, besides being the highest mountain in Guyana proper (the higher Roraima being shared with Brazil and Venezuela), is also the source of the Potaro River, which flows easterly over the majestic Kaieteur Falls which drops 741 ft. / 226 meters vertically making this waterfall one of the wonders of the world. The Potaro River continues easterly over Waratuk and Amatuk Falls passing the mining (gold and diamonds) community of Mahdia, and continues over the Tumatumari Falls on its way to join the mighty Essequibo River.

The ascent of Ayanganna was made in rainy conditions but proved not to be a difficult task for fit soldiers, excepting for a perpendicular section of about 60 feet near the summit which had to be scaled using the vines growing in the pathway.

Upon arrival at the summit, the team stood in low clouds with limited visibility and replaced the flag which had been reduced to tatters by the elements since May 26, 1966. They also cleaned the metal plaque that is cemented in concrete which commemorated the original climb in 1966. Some soldiers used their bayonets to etch their regimental number into the plaque.

On May 26, during their descent, rain began to pour heavily and narrow and quiet streams crossed a day earlier became raging torrents, almost causing the drowning of one soldier.

Upon returning to Chinawying Mission, the team parted company with Mr. Gerry who promised at a later date to take them up Mount Roraima. That promise although accepted, never came into fruition as Lt. Munroe was soon after promoted and transferred as Commander to the Nation's Youth Corps located at Tumatumari. Lt. Munroe's replacement when informed of the Roraima plan, showed no interest.

One side effect of this Ayanganna expedition was an infestation of "Chiggers" (the eggs and larvae deposited by ground mites under the skin of the feet especially the toenails) which all members of the party suffered while relaxing at Chinawying on their way back to Imbimadai airstrip, they were forced to seek medical attention upon their return to Atkinson Base.

On May 15, 1968 Warrant Officers 2 Primo and MacKenzie returned from England. Subsequently, Warrant Officer 2 Richard Cummings and I left for England to attend three courses. These were the All Arms Drill Course, the Senior Non-Commissioned

Officers Weapons and Tactics Course, and the Basic Parachute Course.

The first course was at Caterham, Surrey at the Grenadier Guards Depot. Forty-eight students were in attendance, WO2 Cummings and I being the only two participants who were the only two non-British students in attendance at the course. The course was divided into four squads of twelve students each. The Squads were numbers 1, 2, 3, and 4. I was a member of number 1 Squad and WO2 Cummings was in 2 Squad. The four Squads were trained by four Staff Sergeants from the Grenadier Guards. The Drill Sgt. Major; was Warrant Officer 2 Rigby of the Cold Stream Guards. The course consisted of foot and arms drills; sword drills; pace stick drills; and the art of giving words of command. The course concluded in five weeks with a drill competition.

I was selected to drill number 1 Squad in the drill competition. My drilling instructions to number 1 squad, entailed commands in turning at the halt; marching in slow and quick time; saluting in slow and quick time; and presenting arms. At the conclusion, of the drill competition we assembled in a large auditorium for the closing ceremony. The auditorium was filled with Senior Officers of the Brigade of Guards, relatives and friends of the English students.

The Drill Sergeant Major apprised the audience regarding the intricacies of the course. During the ceremony, it was announced that the number 1 Squad, the Squad that I commanded in the drill competition, had won. I was bestowed the honour of going up on stage to accept the trophy on behalf of the Squad. After that, it was announced that the consensus of all the Drill Instructors and the Drill Sergeant Major; that I was the best student on the course. Once, again, I went onto the stage, and accepted the best student trophy from Drill Sgt. Major Rigby, to the thunderous applause of the large audience. I was congratulated by the Drill Instructors on my accomplishments.

Everyone in attendance at the ceremony celebrated. It was the highlight of my military career, so far.

As soon as, the ceremony concluded, Warrant Officer 2 Richard Cummings and I left for the Infantry Battle School at Brecon in South Wales to attend the Senior Non-Commissioned Officers Tactics and Weapons Course. We travelled by bus to the Infantry Battle School for approximately two hours.

Warrant Officer 2 Compton Hartley Liverpool displaying the two trophies awarded for the Best Student and winning the Drill completion at the All Arms Drill Course, at Caterham, Surrey at the Grenadier Guard Barracks.

Warrant Officer's (WO2) Compton Hartley Liverpool, Oswald Dalgetty, Richard Cummings.

On our arrival, we were interviewed by members of the Directing Staff. One of them was Capt. De Burgh Ferguson, a member of the Black Watch (Royal Highlander) Regiment. He said to me, "You are a three year wonder, your Army is three years old, and you made Warrant Officer 2 in three years. It takes the British Soldier fifteen years to make Warrant Officer. You came to Britain and beat the British at what they do best." Essentially, he warned me that the Tactics and Weapons Course were not a "spit and polish" course". It was the hardest and toughest course in the British Army and it was usually only attended by Sergeants. Warrant Officer 2 (WO2) Richard Cummings and I were the only Warrant Officers there.

There were many training exercises. I was appointed the gunner for all the training exercises. We received our weapons from the arms store. I had to carry the heavy General Purpose

Machine Gun (GPMG) at all times. WO2 Richard Cummings, was designated the radio operator, so he had to carry the heavy A40 radio at all times too. The course consisted of military weapons training, which included the rifle, the light machine gun and the general purpose machine gun. Also, section and platoon battle drills, defensive exercises, withdrawal, and the counter attack. The course concluded in five weeks.

For the next phase of our training, Warrant Officer 2 Richard Cummings and I left for the Army School of Physical Training, to join P Company for Physical Training. The school is located in Aldershot, Hampshire. We travelled by bus for approximately three hours. P Company is a physical training company, and all the members of P Company are Physical Training Instructors.

Our training comprised of numerous gym exercises from 0900 hours until 1500 hours. We ran along the military tank tracks, and maneuvered on the confidence course from plank to plank some forty feet in the air. The duration of the course was two weeks.

At the conclusion of that course, we were sent to the Parachute Training School at the Royal Air Force, RAF Abingdon in Oxfordshire to attend the Basic Parachute Course. It was of five weeks duration training course that encompassed eight parachute jumps. They consisted of the balloon jump; a balloon with a square compartment attached to a rope that is 1000 feet long. At the bottom of the balloon in the compartment there are four soldiers, one instructor and three students. We jumped individually from 1000 feet in the air. One container jump consists of a duffle bag with all the kits, and a rifle attached to your leg, two clean fatigue jumps, one night jump and two more clean fatigue jumps from the C130 Hercules and Argosy troop-carrying aircrafts.

As we were executing our last jump from a C130 Hercules aircraft we observed 2nd Lt. Victor Wilson who had recently graduated from Mons; he had joined the course and was carrying out his first jump at the same time. Immediately, after our last jump, WO2 Cummings and I walked off the drop zone (DZ). We went to the Course Commander's office where we were awarded our parachute wings. It was the completion of all our training. The next day, we travelled by bus to Heathrow airport then boarded a British Airways aircraft and returned to Guyana in late October 1968.

My Company was stationed at Atkinson Field Base, and I was reappointed Company Sgt Major (CSM) for 1 Company. WO2 Richard Cummings was appointed Company Sgt Major CSM for 3 Company and stationed at Atkinson Field Base as well. Capt. Martin Nascimento was the new Officer Commanding 1 Company. In the same month, the Company was preparing to go into Tacama. One week later 1 Company left for Base Tacama to participate in the fourth jungle exercise. The training entailed navigating, building a Base Camp; patrolling from the Base Camp, and river crossing in the jungle. The training concluded in one week and the Company returned to Atkinson Field Base.

Chapter 6

Rupununi Uprising

General Elections were held in November 1968 and the Peoples Nation Congress won the elections by a majority of votes. There was no longer need for a coalition government in Guyana.

During a session in the House of Parliament, an Amerindian (N.K.A Indigenous) Parliamentarian of the Peoples National Congress named Stephen Campbell moved a motion in the House of Parliament requesting that the Makusi, Wapishana and Wai-Wai Indigenous People be granted titles for the land that they had occupied in the Rupununi.

While this motion was being debated in the House, the big ranchers in the Rupununi, Oriello, Gorinsky, McNaughton, Melville, Hart, and Branch all of whom are descendants of 19th Century Scottish settlers, determined that if the Macusi and Wapisiana Indigenous People; were given title to these lands, then the ranchers would lose their stranglehold of five thousand square miles of land, an area as large as the island of Jamaica. As a result, they planned to secede from Guyana and form a Republic of the Rupununi; then make Valerie Hart their Governor. To implement their plans they sent many young Amerindian (N.K.A Indigenous) men to Venezuela for military training. In essence, the Big Ranchers received support, for their decision from the Venezuelan Government. At that time, the Venezuelan Government had placed a claim to two thirds of Guyana's territory that included Essequibo and the Rupununi. The men returned from their training in December 1968. They brought with them caches of arms that included anti-aircraft weapons.

On January 2, 1969, when most Guyanese would have been recovering from the festivities of Old Year's Night /New Year's Eve revelries and New Year's Day, a group of rebels at Lethem attacked the Police Station, shot and killed five (5) policemen - Inspector Whittington Braithwaite, Sergeant James Anderson, Constables James McKenzie, William Norton and one Amerindian (N.K.A Indigenous) Government worker. Capt. Roland DaSilva a Guyana Airways pilot, was having his Dakota Aircraft (DC3 /C-47) loaded with beef at the abattoir and when he heard the shooting quickly closed the doors of the aircraft, taxied away from the abattoir and took off from Lethem. The rebel ranchers arrested District Commissioner Barnwell, his entire staff and all the government workers at Lethem and Annai, in the North Rupununi. They were imprisoned in the abattoir; as well as four black businessmen. As a consequence, they closed Lethem airstrip.

The government in Georgetown was soon able to establish from reports by Roland DaSilva and a Catholic priest who was able to fly his light aircraft out of the area, that most of the airfields in the Rupununi were blocked by the rebels except for one at Manari Ranch some seven miles North East of Lethem which was owned by members of the ranching families who had refused to join the rebellion.

That very day, at about 1400 hours on January 2, 1969; an aircraft landed at Manari airstrip. On board were 2nd Lt Victor Wilson and a section of soldiers from 6 Company. Their mission was to hold the airstrip until they received further orders. At about 1900 hours, a second aircraft, a DC 3 (Dakota) landed under fire at Manari airstrip; on board were Lt. Joseph Singh Officer in Command of 6 Company with approximately fifteen soldiers of his Company; as well as members of the Police Special Branch. The rebels who had fired on them beat a hasty retreat. 6 Company then occupied the guest house at Manari.

On the coast, soldiers returning from their Christmas Holidays furlough were being mobilized at Camp Ayanganna in Georgetown and at Timehri, formerly known as Atkinson Field. Starting at about 1200 hours on 3rd January 1969, Guyana Airways Corporation aircraft and their civilian flight crews began airlifting the main force of the GDF response to the rebellion from Timehri to Manari. This force consisted of 2 Company led by Capt. Vernon Williams, 4 Company led by Capt. Desmond Roberts, and the remainder of 6 Company whose Commander Lt. Joseph Singh had arrived with the advance party the night before. Chief-of-Staff (COS) Colonel Ronald J. Pope along with his Staff Officer Major Ulric Pilgrim also flew in to Manari to take personal command of the operations to oust the rebels from the Rupununi. COS Col. Pope took the three Company Commanders by Guyana Defence Force aircraft on an aerial reconnaissance of Lethem and the surrounding area since prior to January 2, 1969 the GDF had not familiarized itself with the topography of that region.

COS Col. Pope wanted to advance on Lethem with 2 Company and 6 Company since they had the most soldiers on the ground, but the Officer Commanding 6 Company, Lt. Joseph Singh indicated that he wanted more of his soldiers who were still in-transit and were not yet available. Additionally, he wanted 81mm mortars brought in to support the operation, but since it was a counter-insurgence operation COS Col. Pope denied the request. By 1400 hours COS Col. Pope and his Company Commanders had determined that 2 and 4 Company would undertake the advance along the road from Manari to Lethem, and that 6 Company would be held in reserve at Manari.

Shortly thereafter the two companies set out in battle formation arrayed across the savannah straddling the road to Lethem. COS Col. Pope and Maj. Pilgrim rode in a vehicle on the road to keep an eye on progress, behind him were Lt. Col Martindale and his Adjutant Capt. David Granger. Capt. Vernon William's 2 Company with platoons commanded by Lt. Oscar Pollard, 2nd Lt. Kennard Ramphal and 2nd Lt. Maxwell Hinds stayed to the left of the road, while Capt. Desmond Robert's 4 Company with 2nd Lt. Victor Wilson and 2nd Lt. Ian C. Fraser stayed to the right.

By 1700 hours, the formation was on the outskirts of Lethem, and encountering no resistance, COS Col. Pope directed 2 Company to take the Abattoir, Airstrip and commercial complex to the south; while 4 Company was to retake the Government compound, including the Police Station north of the airstrip. Both companies achieved their objectives without resistance or further difficulties. The rebels fled across the Takuta River into Bonfin, Brazil and made their way to Boa Vista; where they sought political asylum.

Prisoners were freed from the Abattoir, and the local residents were encouraged to resume normal activities. By nightfall, not only had order been restored, but further flights from Timerhi were now landing directly at Lethem. One of these took the dead policemen back to Georgetown on its return journey. 6 Company which had discovered a cache of about 20 rebel vehicles hidden in a dry river bed, came up from Manari to join 2 and 4; COS Col. Pope intended to personally clear the North Savannahs the following day with 2 Company. 4 and 6 Company were to continue to protect Lethem and patrol into the South Savannah to ensure there was peace.

Early on the morning of 4th January, COS Col. Pope and Maj. Pilgrim 2 Platoon of 2 Company led by 2nd Lt. Maxwell Hinds boarded a brand new Public Works Department 5 ton dump truck that had only arrived in Lethem in December for "reconnaissance in force" through the North Savannah towards

Annai. COS Col. Pope and Maj. Pilgrim sat in the cab with the driver Pvt. David; 2 Platoon rode in the tray, with hand kerchiefs tied around their nose and mouth, to avoid breathing in the fine savannah dust that enveloped the truck. Following them were Col. Martindale, Capt. Granger, Lt. Pollard's 1 Platoon and 2nd Lt. Ramphal's 3 Platoon; followed behind under Company Commander Capt. Williams to secure Karasabai. A large Indigenous Village in the Pakaraima Mountain Range close to the Brazil border; as well as, the ranches at Karasabai, situated along the road leading to the North Savannah.

For COS Col Pope's party the trip to the North Savannah was uneventful, except that it was noticeable that in all the communities encountered along the way, there were no males over the age of 10 years old. It was later determined, that out of an abundance of caution the Indigenous communities, many of which were in no way involved in the rebellion, had sent their male inhabitants into the hills and jungle bordering the Savannahs, to avoid interaction with both the rebels and also the GDF. It was not until the approach to Annai Government Compound, in the late afternoon that about six male rebels were spotted running off the hill, on which the Police Station stood, into the Savannah with weapons still in hand.

The GDF truck drove up the hill to the Government Compound, where it was discovered that the Police contingent of four led by Cpl. Dover was imprisoned in its own cell. It was also observed that the men who had decamped from the hill upon the GDF approach had disappeared; into one of the copse of jungle (which is a feature of the Rupununi Savannahs). COS Col. Pope ordered 2nd Lt. Hinds to bring in the rebels, and this was duly accomplished, by expediently driving the truck around the copse debussing the men to form a cordon; then sending in a team to sweep through the stand of trees; until the rebels were encountered.

The terrified men immediately gave up, still clutching their weapons; which turned out to be ancient shotguns and one carbine of indeterminate origin. These six men would be among ten misguided rebels arrested, and sent to Georgetown for trial on charges related to the "Rupununi Uprising" as this incident came to be known. All ten men were freed, after the charges against them were dismissed by the presiding magistrate. At Annai it was discovered that Cpl. Dover's young wife and toddler child had run off into the Savannah, when the rebels attacked the Police Station. An extensive search, involving GDF troops and villagers was launched to find Mrs. Dover and her child. Fortunately, on January 6th, the very exhausted missing pair were discovered in the open savannah, some distance from Annai and reunited, with a very relieved Cpl. Dover.

Meanwhile, Lt. Pollard's 1 Platoon, following closely behind COS Col. Pope's party branched off to climb the pass over the mountains to Karasabai valley, arriving there very late on the night of January 4th after an arduous trek. Capt. Vernon Williams and Lt. Kennard Ramphal's platoon had brought up the rear to secure the ranches that the two earlier parties had bypassed. In order to restore calm in the Rupununi, the three main rebel ranchers, Melville, Gorinsky, and Hart ranches were destroyed to prevent them from returning. Consequently, they visited Good Hope and torched the entire ranch thereby burning it to the ground. Further, they moved to Karanambo and they burnt that ranch down too, then Capt. Williams and 2nd Lt. Ramphall poured fuel around the main ranch house to burn it down. As they lifted the torch to burn the house there was a loud explosion; unknowingly, they were pouring aviation fuel. Regrettably, Capt. Vernon Williams and 2nd Lt. Ramphall were severely burnt but they were fortunate to escape with their lives. They were airlifted by GDF Helio-Courier aircraft to Georgetown Hospital for treatment.

Days later, after the Guyana Government held consultations with the Brazilian Embassy in Georgetown, Capt. Carl Morgan, Officer Commanding 5 Company, with half of a platoon (2 sections) from 3 Company under his command, accompanied Senior Police Superintendent, Sam Facey aboard a flight to Lethem. They picked up Deputy District Commissioner Sankar before continuing their air voyage to Boa Vista, Brazil.

Upon arrival in Boa Vista, Police Supt. Facey disembarked the aircraft, to negotiate for the return of the rebels with Brazilian Military authorities, who had taken over the area in response to the insurrection. The Guyanese party was advised, the area was under martial law, and they had no knowledge of an arrangement between the Guyana Government and their Ambassador in Georgetown, they were ordered to leave or be arrested. *They took the prudent course and returned to Lethem.*

The rebel ranchers and their families fled to Santa Elena in Bolivar State, Venezuela. Santa Elena was created to provide political asylum for the Amerindians (N.K.A Indigenous) of the 1969 rebellion. There is a standing order in Venezuela, to grant political asylum to any Amerindian (N.K.A Indigenous) from the Western side of the Essequibo River in Guyana - whom they consider to be Venezuelan citizens.

Calm was restored to the Rupununi within a few days of the GDF intervention. Most of the troops, who took part in the operation, were withdrawn within weeks. As a result of a very successful operation, the Guyana Defence Force established four permanent locations in the Rupununi. They are Lethem, Good Hope, Annai and Orinduk. Accordingly, 6 Company was left as the occupying Company under the command of Lieutenant Aubrey Featherstone.

The Guyana Defence Force first Chief -of- Staff

Lieutenant Colonel Ronald James Pope, a British citizen was appointed Commanding Officer of the newly formed 1st Battalion of the Guyana Defence Force (GDF) in December 1965. Immediately before coming to Guyana, he was a Staff Officer with the British Army on the Rhine (BAOR) in Germany and was promoted to the rank of Lieutenant Colonel to be Commanding Officer of the GDF.

In May 1967, he was granted an extraordinary extension in service through 1969 during which time he was promoted to the rank of Colonel and the first Chief of Staff of the GDF, a position he held through March 1969. Born in 1924, he was commissioned into the South Wales Borders Regiment of the British Army in 1943 and started his Military career with the 1st Battalion, The Monmouthshire Regiment in Palestine, Middle East (a British Protectorate after the First World War that was carved out of the former Ottoman Empire.) before becoming Adjutant of 2nd Battalion in 1947.

In 1950 he re-joined the 1st Battalion in Eritrea, Horn of Africa as Adjutant, an appointment he filled with memorable distinction and efficiency.

He was an instructor at Eaton Hall Officer Training School from 1954-55, and shortly after attending the Staff College in 1956. This was followed by two years in Malta and a further year as a Company Commander with the 1st Battalion in Minden, Germany.

In 1961, he graduated from Joint Services Staff College Latimer, he then returned to Minden, Germany for a very successful tour as Brigade Major of 11th Infantry Brigade.

He was the epitome of the practical regimental soldier who was at his happiest in the field. His loyalty to and affection for his regiment was paramount and he was a staunchly patriotic Welshman. An active sportsman, and particularly keen on athletics, boxing, rugby and riding, he had a passion for physical fitness which at times impressed and yet doubly encouraged many of his Officers.

Considered by many to be serious - a description he himself would never deny - he was to those who knew him well a warm hearted, generous and steadfast friend with a keen social awareness and a hidden sense of humour. Unknown to many, he had undisclosed talents as the author of several children's books and a composer of military marches.

In March 1969 Guyana Defence Soldiers lined both sides of the road in Camp Ayanganna, the lines started from the Officers mess at the back to the front gate. Colonel Ronald James Pope was standing in his land rover with a continuous salute; as he was being push out of the compound by the Officers. Colonel Pope was finally leaving the Guyana Defence Force. He was the last of the expatriate soldiers, who was returning to the United Kingdom. At the end of his tour in Guyana, he was rewarded with the honour of St. Companion of the Order of St. Michael and St. George (CMG).

Upon his departure, Lieutenant Colonel Clarence Price was appointed the Chief of Staff with the rank of Colonel, and Lieutenant Colonel Robert B. Stephenson was appointed Commanding Officer for the 1st Battalion

L to R: Officers- Cecil Martindale, Oscar Pollard (hidden), Asad Ishoof, Maxwell Hinds, David Granger, CV Bowen, Watson Joseph, Ulric Pilgrim, Harry Hinds, Richard Fraser, Joe Singh, Godwin McPherson, Vernon Williams, Desmond Roberts, Fairbairn Liverpool, Keith Dyer, Penny Stuart-Young, Unidentified, Arthur Benfield (Partial profile).

Colonel Clarence Price

The Chief of Staff Brigadier General Colonel Price congratulates Warrant Officer 2 Compton Hartley Liverpool on being awarded the first Military Service Medal for Valour on May 26, 1970.

Chapter 7

Operation-Climax, New River

In July 1969 Guyana Airways pilots were flying over the New River Triangle. The New River Triangle is Guyana's eastern border with Suriname; it is mainly jungle and has many tributaries of the New River. The pilots took photographs of a Dutch camp on Guyana's territory and these photographs were submitted to Prime Minister Linden Forbes Sampson Burnham.

Consequently, he ordered the Guyana Defence Force to mount an operation. The operation was code named "Operation Climax." Colonel Robert B. Stephenson Commanding Officer of the 1st Battalion ordered elements of 1 Company, 2 Company, 3 Company, the Mortar Platoon and the Reconnaissance Platoon to move to Tacama for training. Tacama is the Guyana Defence Force Battle School in the Ituni Savannahs of the Lower Berbice River.

These five sub units converged at Tacama on August 16, 1969. Eighty four soldiers were selected for the operation. They were divided into twelve sections of seven soldiers in each section. Each section was commanded by an Officer, a Warrant Officer or a Sergeant. The Company Commanders were Captain Martin Nascimento and Captain Asad Ishoof, and I was the Company

Sergeant Major. The battle drills training commenced with Section and Platoon attack exercises.

On the morning of August 17, 1969, two Guyana Airways DHC-6 De Havilland (Twin Otter) aircrafts landed at Tacama airstrip. The aircrafts were flown by Captain Roland DaSilva, Captain Michael Chan- A-Sue, Captain Anthony Mekdeci, and Captain Phillip Jardim. The doors and the seats of the aircraft were removed. The Twin Otter aircraft has the capacity to accommodate thirty passengers. The pilots exited their respective aircrafts. Shortly afterwards, they held a consultation with the Guyana Defence Force High Command.

When the meeting was concluded, the pilots instructed four soldiers to erect a small tent that represented a house on the right side of the airstrip. As soon as the tent was erected, all the soldiers that were selected for the Operation began the boarding and exiting the aircraft training exercises, and attacking an adversary camp.

As I stood with the Company Commander, watching the troops going through their training exercises, I was wondering what role I would play in the Operation. At that juncture, the Company Commander then told me, the Guyana Airways pilots requested that someone had to be placed in the nose compartment of the aircraft; with a machine gun to protect them from adversarial ground fire. The Company Commander informed me that I was selected to perform the task of an Aerial gunner. (An aerial gunner is a member of an air crew who operates flexible-mounted machine guns in an aircraft; performs aerial gunner functions as dictated by aircraft and mission type during integrated air or ground operations.) I complied with the order and decided to inspect the aircraft. I saw a compartment with a door and latch on the outside of the aircraft fuselage and below the flight cabin (cockpit); I was advised that passengers normally store their packages there, when they are flying into the interior of Guyana.

The pilots opened the compartment; I climbed into the compartment and placed myself in a sitting position; with my back against the wall, and my legs were fully extended. When I was solidified in the position, the pilots closed the compartment. After that was accomplished, we went flying around Tacama practising several aerial tactics. The manoeuvres consisted of gliding from the air to the airstrip, landing in reverse thrusts and taking off again. These drills concluded in approximately one hour. Subsequently, we returned to the airstrip it was our final aerial training for the day. After we landed, the pilots opened the compartment for me to get out. When I got out, they asked me how I felt. *"I said okay, but it was dark in the compartment."*

Shortly thereafter, Colonel Clarence Price arrived on the Guyana Defence Force Helio Courier aircraft. Colonel Price was accompanied by Lionel B. Sullivan, a technician from Guyana Technical Institute. He conversed with the pilot for a few minutes; then proceeded to the front of the aircraft; removed the nose cone and placed it on the ground. Once, it was removed a flat aluminium plate about four feet square and a quarter of an inch thick was visible. He examined the exposed front of the plane, to determine if it was viable for his plans.

He then cut four slots in the fibreglass bulkhead of the aircraft with a saw. These slots were about twelve inches by six inches in length; they were two up and two down. He riveted transparent celluloid over the four slots and made four windows. He then proceeded to cut a hole in the centre of the plate and placed the barrel of a General Purpose Machine Gun (GPMG) through the hole. Another hole was cut in the leatherette he brought with him, and strapped to the barrel of the machine gun; then he riveted the leatherette unto the aluminium plate. Once this was completed, he tested the weapon to ascertain its functionality; to manoeuvre left and right, or up and down. Throughout, the testing, I was outside the aircraft observing its setup and manoeuvres, to confirm the efficiency of the movements.

Armed with belted 7.62mm ammunition over my left shoulder, I climbed back into the aircraft and loaded the weapon. The Pilots closed the compartment and we went flying around Tacama again. There was an intercom between the Pilots and myself. As we flew around the Savannah, they were identifying targets for me and I was firing at them, for a period of time before they terminated the training exercise.

On the morning of August 18th 1969, we were assembled outside of our Barrack rooms; awaiting the arrival of Prime Minister Linden Forbes Sampson Burnham (LFSB). Later, he arrived at Tacama Battle School accompanied by Captain Fairbairn Liverpool, Adjutant of the 1st Battalion. After the Prime Minister disembarked the aircraft, he was immediately taken to an office for a conference with Guyana Airways Pilots and the Guyana Defence Force High Command. He was briefed about the training and the personnel that were selected for the mission.

When the meeting was concluded, we were still assembled in front of the two Barrack rooms. I paraded all eighty four soldiers on the Operation unto the Parade Square. The Prime Minister came out of the office and stood on a rostrum; he used a mega phone and gave us the orders for the mission. He told us that soldiers from the Suriname Army had occupied Guyana's territory in the New River Triangle. They had built a camp and were in the process of building an airstrip. He said "our mission was to go into the New River and remove them from Guyana's territory." *"He stated; if a small nation like Suriname could occupy our Country and we do nothing about it, what would we do if larger countries to our south Brazil and west Venezuela did the same?"*

The Prime Minister gave us the mission and came down from the rostrum. He was introduced to all eighty four members of the operation and shook their hands. When he came to me, he said *"Liverpool do you know that you are likely to be killed on this operation?"* I said *"Comrade Leader, I am being paid to do the job that I am doing and if getting killed is part of it, so be it."* He said *"that is what he wanted to hear, take out the Dutch soldiers and he will visit us the next day."*

Once, the introductions were completed, he returned to the office for lunch with the Pilots and the Guyana Defence Force Officers. Afterwards, the Prime Minister left Tacama Battle School. Accordingly, the soldiers returned to their barrack rooms. Tacama Battle School was closed down, and no one was allowed to leave or enter the Base. All the soldiers who were not on the operation were confined to their barrack rooms; there was complete radio silence on the base for approximately forty-eight hours.

At around 1400 hours the same day, Phase 1 of the operation commenced. We left our barrack rooms and assembled outside, On the Base, there were four, three ton Bedford trucks; all eighty four soldiers boarded the trucks that left Tacama Battle School by road for the MacKenzie airstrip. At the airstrip there were two Guyana Airways Dakota aircrafts waiting. The soldiers boarded the aircrafts, and the two aircrafts took off for the staging area of Apoteri.

Apoteri is a small community made up of Indigenous Wapashinas, Makushi and Patomona people located near the confluence of the Rupununi River (upper Takutu) with the upper Essequibo River. It's located approximately 30 miles East by North (EbN) of Annai; 10 miles North-Northwest (NNW) of Kumaka; and 90 miles Southeast (SE) 'to' New River/Camp Jaguar or North West (NW)from Camp Jaguar.

Simultaneously, Colonel Price, Lieutenant Colonel Stephenson, Major Pilgrim, Captain Fairbairn Liverpool, Captain Nasimento, Captain Ishoof and I left Tacama in two Twin Otter aircrafts. Additionally, we were accompanied by the Guyana Defence Force Helio Courier aircraft to Apoteri as well. We disembarked the aircrafts and observed the soldiers who were there before us, and were already in the process of preparing for the mission. That afternoon heavy gunfire could be heard over the Rupununi River, as the soldiers test fired their weapons. When the test firing practice was completed, they cleaned and assembled their weapons, pack their kits and assembled them in Company groups

Dinner was 1600 hours which consisted of boiled rice with corn beef or sardines. After dinner that evening, most of us slept in our sleeping bags under the stars; some of the officers and I slept under the wings of the aircrafts, and the others slept in the aircrafts. Fortunately the weather was good because there was no rain. Reveille was at 0300 hours on August 19th and at 0400 hours the soldiers had their breakfast - hot tea and soda biscuits.

After breakfast each soldier was issued with 120 rounds (20 rounds X 6 magazines) of live ammunition. At 0430 hours the Guyana Airways pilots were now dressed in the Guyana Defence Force uniforms and wearing the rank of majors and armed with sterling sub-machine guns (SMG's) for the purpose of the mission. The Guyana Airways pilots asked the GDF pilot Captain Lambert Smith to 'go up' in his aircraft; to check the cloud coverage over the area, but he refused. He said that *"his contract did not involve participating in a war furthermore he was a Trinidadian and he was no fly boy."* Major Phillip Jardim then took the Guyana Defence Force aircraft and went up to check the cloud coverage, on his return he concurred with the other pilots that he observed clear skies towards the area of operation (AO).

This signalled the commencement of Phase 2 of the operation. Forty-two soldiers boarded the two aircrafts; in the first aircraft flown by Capt. Roland Da Silva and his co-pilot Capt. Michael Chan-a-Sue were twenty one (21) soldiers – 7 X 3 teams that made up the first chalk (a group of soldiers that deploy from a single aircraft) and the team leaders, Lieutenant Marcus Munroe, Lieutenant Keith Dyer and Sergeant Joel Simmons; also sitting at the door of the aircraft was Captain Martin Nascimento. Each section was made up of members of the Reconnaissance Platoon.

In the second aircraft flown by Capt. Philip Jardim and his co-pilot Capt. Anthony Mekdeci were 2nd Lieutenant Milton Britton and his section, Warrant Officer 2 Richard Cummings and his section, Sergeant Rocky Mohammed and his section, other members of the Mortar Platoon with their mortar tubes, mortar base plates and their 81mm mortar bombs; sitting at the door of the aircraft was Captain Harry Hinds Officer Commanding the Mortar Platoon.

At 0515 hours, I climbed into the compartment of the first aircraft loaded my weapons which included my Self Loading Rifle (SLR). I received good wishes from the Chief of Staff, the Battalion Commanders and other Senior Officers. The pilots closed the compartment and I was left alone with my thoughts. In essence, I was thinking about the mission ahead.

Warrant Officer – Compton Hartley Liverpool in front of bunker.

At 0530 hours the two aircrafts took off from Apoteri and climbed high into the morning skies. The flight to the New River Triangle, approximately 90 miles South East (SE) of Apoteri took approximately half an hour. As we began our descent into the New River Triangle the pilot turned off their engines and the aircrafts started gliding towards the ground. At the outset, I observed the Dutch camp; then secondly, I observed the airstrip. The airstrip was covered with many forty-five gallons petro drums and surveyors sticks; there was also a small bulldozer on the airstrip; also, on the right side of the airstrip was a small hut. When we were about two thousand feet from the ground the pilots turned on the engine.

As the aircraft was approaching its landing on the air strip just as the sun was breaking the horizon, I observed six Dutch soldiers ran out from the hut with their weapons. Before they could raise their weapons, I immediately opened fire with my

General Purpose Machine Gun (GPMG.) I fired the first shots in defence of Guyana; causing the first two soldiers to drop to the ground, when the others realized what was happening, they all threw themselves to the ground, and started crawling quickly into the direction of the nearby jungle. What saved them; is at the same time the aircraft landed and threw me off my aim; by the time I recommenced firing they had all crawled into the jungle. At that point, I saw Lieutenant Marcus Munroe and his section of soldiers all of whom had disembarked while the aircraft was still travelling down the airstrip towards the water's edge (the airstrip is approximately 40 feet above the river). He was waving frantically at me to stop firing; so I acted in accordance with his directive. His team and that on Lt. Dyer's team ran down the airstrip and cleared the hut; they removed the drums, and sticks from the airstrip. The aircraft then taxied down the airstrip away from the river towards the opposite end to position itself for take-off on its return voyage to Apoteri.

Thereafter, at the debriefing, I learned the other team led by Sergeant Joel Simmons that covered the trail that led to and from the airstrip, and the river bank at the end of the airstrip, would soon after taking up their positions and while looking down the trail observed a Willy's jeep with five (5) uniformed Surinamese soldiers armed with M1 Saginaw .30 caliber Carbines that had just turned the corner at the bottom of the trail at a high rate of speed heading up-hill towards their direction while the aircraft was still preparing for take-off. Separated by a distance of 40 yards, they, Joel Simmons and Clairmonte Griffith opened fire with their Self Loading Rifle's (SLR) above their heads, prompting them to stop, reverse, and return back into the camp area.

After that action, the airstrip was fully secured permitting the aircraft to depart safely thus allowing the second and subsequent Guyana Airways Corporation (GAC) aircrafts and the GDF's Helio-Courier to land and take off at will.

The second aircraft arrived and the soldiers disembarked. At this stage, we now had forty-two men on the ground. The two aircrafts had returned to Apoteri for the second batch of forty-two men; this group was led by Captain Asad Ishoof.

When we landed, the propellers of the aircraft were still running. As the forty-two soldiers were boarding the two aircrafts, the pilot opened the compartment of the aircraft that I was in briefly; so that the Chief of Staff could communicate with me. The Chief of Staff and the Battalion Commander came to the aircraft; then I enlightened them, with respect to what had occurred at the New River Triangle. The pilots quickly closed the compartment, and we were airborne again for the New River Triangle.

During the second flight to the New River Triangle, I felt blood running from my right ears along my face, from the pressure of being in the compartment for a while. When we landed, I apprised the pilots that I was leaving the aircraft, because at that phase, my task was over. Hence, I left the aircraft with my rifle and joined the attacking force. After I left the aircraft, Lance Corporal Ramcharitar entered the compartment and assumed the role of handling the General Purpose Machine Gun (GPMG.) The two aircrafts left for Apoteri for the soldiers' kits.

The Dutch camp was approximately four hundred yards from the airstrip in the jungle, and also there was a trail leading towards the camp. On the left hand side of the trail were Captain Asad Ishoof and his men, and on the right side were Lieutenant Marcus Munroe and his men. The Dutch soldiers were firing at us at first, but the Mortar Platoons zeroed in on their camp and started dropping the mortar bombs; as we skirmished through the jungle. Lieutenant Marcus Munroe and his men were the first to enter the camp. However, the soldiers and the Djukas/Maroons had fled down to the river as we converged on the outskirts of the camp.

Note: History has revealed that the Djukas were imported from Africa during the slave trade period to work as labourers on the sugar plantations of Suriname but who escaped into the interior to make their homes in a largely undeveloped area.

The camp was about forty feet above the river on high ground. There were about thirty soldiers in six long boats. Two of the long boats had travelled down river with soldiers and Djukas; two of them had travelled up river, and the other two boats were still trying to start their engines.

Captain Ishoof, ordered the Guyana Defence Force soldiers to hold their fire. Essentially, our mission was to remove them from Guyana's territory. Evidently, the two boats that had travelled up river were proceeding to another camp that was approximately ten miles, but when they noticed that we were not firing at those below us they turned back; by then the two boats below us had started their engines and all six boats went down river to a Dutch camp on their side of the border that was in close proximity.

Profoundly, we accomplished an effective and triumphant mission. The Dutch flag was lowered and the Golden Arrowhead was raised in victory. Consequently, the Guyana Defence Force had taken camp El Tigre from the Dutch soldiers and we renamed it "Camp Jaguar." As a result, Company positions were allocated around the camp, and clearing patrols were sent into the jungle and Sentries were posted to guard the airstrip. With the success of the mission, there was one initial casualty. Captain Martin Nascimento reported that when the aircraft landed, he fell out and the rear wheel ran over his midriff. As a consequence of the accident, he was left out of battle (LOB) and he remained on the airstrip. When the two aircrafts returned with the soldiers' kits from Apoteri that afternoon; Captain Martin Nascimento left in one of the two aircrafts en-route to Timerhi.

The Camp was located approximately 400+/- yards from the airstrip. It had a separate housing for the Djukus, mainly a long range zinc covered shelter with cots about four feet apart from each with twenty plus cots on each side of the shelter. A few underground fortified bunkers were found.

In addition, there was a food storage area (bond), a small armory with a few MI Saginaw Carbines .30 caliber, and a small mess hall for dining. Moreover, there was an American built Willy's Jeep in the Camp.

The Dutch soldiers had left a storage area that was filled with rations. They were cooking when we attacked the camp. The soldiers ate the food that they were cooking; along with the cans of foodstuff that were in the store room. The Clearing Patrols returned, after clearing the camp and nearby bushes. Thereafter, the Sentries were withdrawn into the camp. That night we had what was known as a "Baptism of Fire" all the soldiers open fire with their weapons into the jungle for one minute, as well as the mortars. The next day patrols were sent into the jungle and we began digging bunkers, one patrol led by Warrant Officer 2 Richard Cummings returned with a Dutch soldier by the name of Margo Van Dams with his hands tied behind his back he was eighteen years old at the time.

Later that day the two twin otter aircrafts returned with rations and service support for the location. On board were Major Cecil Martindale, Captain Vibart Boodhoo, Lieutenant Joseph Singh, Warrant Officer 2 Dhalgetty and others including Lance Corporal Edward Smith. Lance Cpl Smith 'hot-wired' the abandoned vehicle at the location which was immediately used to transport visitors from the air strip to the camp and vice versa. It was also used in pulling logs from cut trees in the making of bunkers – military fortification designed to protect people or valued materials from falling bombs or other attacks.

Later that afternoon they left with the Dutch prisoner for Timerhi. On day three of the operation as we continued digging bunkers a fighting patrol of thirty men led by Lieutenant Marcus Munroe left to attack the Dutch camp down river. After walking a day and a night, orders were received from Guyana Defence Force Headquarters to abort the mission. Therefore, these orders were transferred to Lieutenant Marcus Munroe by radio and by the Guyana Defence Force aircraft flying overhead. They were about two miles from the Dutch camp when the mission was aborted. We had one fatality, Private Ramsingh who was killed when a tree he was cutting for the making of bunkers fell upon him.

One week later Prime Minister Linden Forbes Sampson Burnham arrived at the Camp with many foreign and national journalists. I met Prime Minister Forbes Burnham for the second time. He commended me for my performance on the operation. The entire group toured the Camp and later that day they left Camp Jaguar. After one month we handed over Camp Jaguar to 4 Company. All participants in the four chalks received the Jaguar Medal!

Chapter 8

First Local Officer's Cadet Course

On January 1st 1970, the Guyana Defence Force commenced its first Officer Cadet course. This was a five month course that entailed all aspects of military training. It was conducted by 2nd Lieutenant Victor Wilson, and the Training Officer was Captain Oscar Pollard. Some of the Officer Cadets on the course were George Maynard, Raymond Seopaul, Calvin Clarke, Hilton Mac David, Cecil Austin, Leroy Benn, Lennox DeCruz, Maurice Hendricks and Errol Maynard, a student from St Kitts Defence Force. On 15th of January, Officer Cadets Calvin Clarke and Hilton Mc David were selected to attend the MONS Officer Cadet School in England, and on January 20th they departed for England.

Also on January 15th 1970, I was a member of a Guard of Honour at the opening of Parliament. As we awaited the arrival of Prime Minister Forbes Burnham, the names of a number of Guyanese who were awarded national honours was announced over the public address system, then I heard my name being mentioned amongst the recipients. In addition, it was announced at the same sitting of the National Assembly in the House of Parliament, that Guyana would become a Cooperative Republic and on 23rd of February 1970. Justice Arthur Chung was to be appointed Guyana's first Ceremonial President.

Venezuela's Aggression at Eteringbang, Cuyuni River

As Guyana was preparing, for the celebrations of the birth of its Cooperative Republic the 23rd of February 1970; Venezuelans on Ankoko Island began shelling Eteringbang Village, including the Police Station with machine gun and mortar fire on the 21st of February. Lieutenant Maxwell Hinds the officer commanding the location; with a platoon of 6 Company plus a detachment of troops from the Engineer Corps, radioed the situation to the Guyana Defence Force Headquarters. The matter was reported to Prime Minister Linden Forbes S. Burnham, who ordered that the GDF should hold its fire. The Venezuelans continued firing at the location at dawn, midday and twilight on the 22nd. All civilians and police ranks, were evacuated by foot over the mountains towards Ekereku Village on the afternoon of the 22nd.

On the 23rd February during the noon bombardment, four Venezuelan soldiers were observed setting up a mortar, on the Venezuelan side of the Cuyuni in clear site and range of the GDF troops on the heights above Eteringbang. Lt. Hinds requested permission from GDF Headquarters to return fire, by targeting the Venezuelan mortar team on the beach who had by then casually commenced lobbing high explosive mortars unto the GDF position. The mortar shells, mainly exploded high up in the trees and no casualties occurred, among the troops deployed in bunkers and communication trenches on the hillside.

Captain Michael Leitch, General Staff Officer 3 at GDF Headquarters, was at the other end of the radio; and he ordered Lt. Hinds to withdraw from the location. Lt. Hinds led his men along the Cuyuni River towards Ekereku. Capt. Joseph Singh Officer Commanding 6 Company was at Baramadan. He radioed GDF Head Quarters and reported that the Venezuelan bombers were circling overhead with their bomber doors open.

If Lt. Maxwell Hinds had killed those four Venezuelan soldiers, it was likely that Venezuelans would have claimed justification in escalating the incident into an invasion, seizure of more territory; or other punitive action against Guyana. As it was, no harm befell any Venezuelan, and Guyana was able through diplomatic means to bring a halt to the bombardment and overflying of its territory.

Guided by Boatman Johnson, Lt. Hinds' unit climbed the Ekereku Plateau in the vicinity of Sakaika Falls three days after leaving Eterinbang. On the fourth day they reached Ekereku Camp. The police and civilian party also arrived there by different route around the same time. Captain Ishoof and members of 1 Company were sent to Kamarang by Guyana Airways Dakota aircraft, to re-occupy the location at Eteringbang, as Lt. Hinds and his men had left. Kamarang is the connecting point to Eteringbang. From there, they were planning to continue their journey, by trekking on foot to the location.

As their plans progressed, they realized that the terrain was rough and not conducive for that type of journey. For that reason, 2nd Lieutenant Milton Britton and a number of soldiers from 1 Company, volunteered to be flown back into Eteringbang by GDF Heio Courier aircraft. The pilot of the aircraft was Lt. Frank Vieira. They landed at Eteringbang airstrip, and made their way back to the location and re-occupied it. Subsequently, the other soldiers were shuttled by GDF aircraft to the location. The Venezuelans did not re-commence firing; by the end of the day 1 Company had converged at Eteringbang.

Guyana Defence Force moves to the North West District (Region 1).

The GDF made the decision to occupy all the airstrips in the North West Region. 2 Company lead by Captain Robert Mitchell, left Base Timerhi for Mabaruma. I was a member of that Company. We landed at Mabaruma airstrip in two Guyana Airways Dakota aircrafts. We set up a location at the Mabaruma airstrip. The next day, I left with a Section of soldiers in two outboard motor boats for Port Kaituma, where there is an airstrip.

In approximately one hour, we reached Port Kaituma; disembarked the motor boats and trekked by foot to a place called "The Bottom Floor" where the Port Kaituma airstrip is located. Immediately, we blocked the airstrip with lumber and other large objects from the surrounding areas and guarded it. Mike Semple, a local resident who had a guest house and a night spot; gave us two rooms in his guest house to be used for our Barracks. We guarded the airstrip by day and occupied the guest house at night. During the same period, Captain Desmond Roberts and members of 4 Company landed at Matthews Ridge and they occupied a number of buildings up on the Ridge.

Five days later we were uplifted by GDF aircraft from Port Kaituma and taken to Baramita. Baramita is located South West of Matthews Ridge and it is the furthest point west in the Barima-Waini Region where Guyana's Border intersects with the Venezuelan border. There was a long airstrip at Baramita with a Guyana Airways Corporation office with an agent by the name of Mr. Baird, and he was also a gold miner. The Guyanese and the Venezuelan miners' criss-cross the border in search of gold. Five days later, we were uplifted from Baramita and returned to Base Timerhi. Consequently, the GDF established two locations one at Mabaruma and one at Matthews Ridge.

Chapter 9

Investiture Ceremony and Awards

On May 26th 1970, there was an investiture ceremony at Guyana House, for all the Guyanese who were awarded National Honours. They assembled at Guyana House to be presented with their accolades by President Arthur Chung. Prime Minister Linden Forbes Burnham was presented with Guyana's highest honour the "Order of Excellence" Brigadier Clarence Price received the "Military Service Star" the four Guyana Airways pilots Capt. Roland DaSilva received the "Cacique Crown of Valour" Captain Michael Chan-A-Sue, Captain Phillip Jardim and Captain Anthony Mekdeci received the "Golden Arrow Head of Courage" and I was presented with the "Military Service Medal for Valour". During my presentation, Chancellor Sir Edward Luckhoo announced to the *dignitaries and guests* that my medal epitomised "Bravery beyond the normal call of duty".

Virtus est militis decus (Valor is the soldier's honor).

Warrant Officer Compton Hartley Liverpool receiving the "Military Service Medal for Valour." from President Arthur Chung. Chancellor Sir Edward Luckhoo is standing behind the President.

The first Office Cadet Course was completed at the end of the month of May 1970. Seven Officer Cadets were commissioned with the rank of 2nd Lieutenant, 2nd Lieutenant George Maynard was adjudged the "Best Cadet" and 2nd Lieutenant Errol Maynard from St. Kitts-Nevis (West Indies) Defence Force was the runner up.

In July 1970, the second Officer Training Course commenced and Lieutenant Victor Wilson was the course officer. Some of the Officer Cadets were Michael Atherly, Perry Foo, Lambert Marks, Ronald Pickering, Patrick Boyce, James (Jimmy) King, Edmond Joseph, George Davidson, and Malcolm Williams. The course concluded in January 1971, with the Commissioning of these Officers to the rank of 2ⁿᵈ Lieutenant George Davidson was adjudged the "Best Cadet" and 2ⁿᵈ Lieutenant Scott Hendricks from St. Kitts-Nevis (West Indies) Defence Force was the runner up. Years later, the best cadet was awarded a "Baton of Honor" and the runner up the "Under Officer."

Soldier of the Year and Promotions

In December 1970, I was named "Soldier of The Year." To date, it is the first and only time this recognition was ever awarded in the Guyana Defence Force. The acknowledgment was published in the December edition, of the Guyana Defence Force Scarlet Beret magazine. On January 1ˢᵗ 1971, Warrant Officers Richard Cummings, Dyal Panday and I were commissioned with the ranks of Substantive Lieutenants. As a result of us being promoted to Senior Lieutenants; this caused confusion amongst some of the Lieutenants in the GDF. I was the most senior Lieutenant, because of my senior regimental number. One of the Lieutenants even wrote the Chief of Staff Brigadier General Clarence Price registering his disappointment with the promotions. Evidently, it was to no avail, and did not change the status quo of the promotions.

On March 2ⁿᵈ 1971, the GDF initiated its first Junior Officers Staff Course conducted by Captain Harry Hinds and the training comprised of staff duties in the field. Of the three of us who were commissioned, I was the only one selected to attend the course which concluded in five weeks. In April 1971, the GDF commenced its first Junior Command and Tactics Course. Again I was the only one selected of three who were commissioned to attend the course. It was conducted by Lieutenant Victor Wilson, and concluded in five weeks. Both of these courses were at Base Timerhi location. In the month of May the same year, I was posted to 2 Company, and assumed the command of

Bases at Paruima Mission on the Kamarang River, and Kurotoko on the Cuyuni River for the duration of two months.

On August 1ˢᵗ in the same year, the GDF conducted its first Escape and Evasion Course for all the Junior Officers at Tacama Battle School. We were trained by Capt. Marcus Munroe and Major Carl Morgan; in methods of Interrogation, Escape and Evasion and other related tactics. On August 5ᵗʰ after four days of training, we assembled during the afternoon at Ituni Creek; it is a distance of five miles from the Battle School. The "Escape" was scheduled to start there the next morning. The cooks were preparing a "hangie supper." The "hangie supper" consisted of wild meat, accarei (agouti), labba (spotted cavy), venison, iguana, even caiman tail, and various herbs from the jungle. I did not participate in the supper or the Escape and Evasion exercise. The reason being, the orders that were received from the Chief of Staff Clarence Price; stating that he was sending an aircraft for me to return to Georgetown. A GDF Highlander aircraft arrived at Tacama, to transport me to Georgetown. During the trip, I was wondering what could have gone wrong as I left Tacama.

As soon as we landed at Ogle airport, there was a GDF vehicle waiting to take me to the Chief of Staff. When I met with him; he informed me to report to Mr. Oscar Henry, Permanent Secretary to the Prime Minister; at the Office of The Prime Minister, located in the Public Building on Monday morning at 0900 hours. I reported to Mr. Oscar Henry; after a short conversation I was ushered into Prime Minister Linden Forbes Burnham's office. The Prime Minister immediately relieved my anxiety; by offering me snacks of patties, stuffed eggs, cheese sandwiches and homemade drink.

Subsequently, Prime Minister Linden Forbes Burnham and Mr Oscar Henry questioned me intensively about the Guyana Defence Force. Essentially, they wanted information about four Senior Officers. They were Lieutenant Colonels Cecil Martindale, Robert Stephenson, Claude Bowen and Ulric Pilgrim. I had served with these Officers in the Volunteer Force; so I gave favourable responses to the questions asked by Prime Minister Burnham. His last question was *"How the soldiers would feel if Lieutenant Colonel Pilgrim was appointed Force Commander of the Guyana Defence Force."* Lieutenant Colonel Pilgrim was my squaddie from the Volunteer Force; we always had a good relationship so I gave a positive answer. I was then sworn to secrecy by Prime Minister Burnham.

At 1200 hours that day, I was the lone passenger flying back into Tacama, by then it was too late for me to participate in the Escape and Evasion exercise; so I became a member of the Hunter Force. Later, I was told that 2nd Lieutenants Michael Atherley and Malcolm Williams conducted themselves satisfactorily, when they were captured and interrogated. After the Escape and Evasion exercise, no one asked me any questions and I did not volunteer any information. However, the Chief of Staff Brigadier Clarence Price had leaked information that I had gone to see Prime Minister Forbes Burnham, for a private meeting. Consequently, I was not the most popular person in the GDF at that time.

Return to New River

In October 1971, I was sent to the New River Triangle location with a Platoon of soldiers from 2 Company. We were dressed in civilian clothes, the soldiers at Camp Jaguar were also dressed in civilian clothes, and they also carried their weapons in sand bags. The Government of Guyana and the Government of Suriname had made an agreement to demilitarize the area. There were many farmers at the location including two Americans; one was Edward Washington and in later years he was known as Rabbi Washington, the other farmer was Paul Adams, and in later years he would become a member of the Guyana National Service with the rank of Major.

My location was not at Camp Jaguar; it was four miles up the river at Camp Puma. Already at the location, was Lieutenant Maxwell Hinds Officer Commanding the Reconnaissance Platoon, and a platoon of soldiers. Lieutenant Hinds was making mortar base plates positions and digging bunkers. I took over the location from Lieutenant Hinds. My main task, was to cut down the under bush in the jungle to build an airstrip.

In my platoon, there were many good hunters, and in one day they shot and killed nine wild hogs. The meat was too much for the location so I decided to take some of the meat to the soldiers at Camp Jaguar. For my trip to the camp, I had a small fibreglass boat and a boatman by the name of Mr. Moses. After delivering the pork to Camp Jaguar, I left on my return journey back to Camp Puma. I had just entered the mouth of the New River; then I observed two Dutch long boats emerging from behind two islets (Small Islands) there were four Dutch soldiers in each of the boats. They were travelling to my right and to my left about ten feet away.

As we made our way up river, the Dutch soldiers' boats then started circling my boat and caused it to bubble in the ripple of their waves. I did not know their intention; therefore, I did not hesitate to find out. I swiftly picked up my sub-machine gun and cradle it in my arms; when they saw my reaction; both boats abruptly stopped encircling, my boat and went between two islands and disappeared. Afterwards, I continued my journey back to the camp.

When I arrived at my camp, I commanded the soldier to "stand to" then I explained the situation to them. The soldiers lined the bank of the river with their weapons in full view. The Dutch soldiers had to pass our location to get to theirs. As they were passing, I observed they had a different mind-set, because they were smiling and waving. At that instance, I realised that a serious confrontation had been averted. I completed my assigned tasks, and in December 1971, I handed over that location to 2nd Lieutenant George Maynard and his platoon.

Chapter 10

Pivotal Changes in the Guyana Defence Force

On January 1st 1972, it was a pivotal year in the Guyana Defence Force, Lieutenant Colonels Cecil Martindale, Robert Stephenson, and Claude Bowen, were all sent back to their civilian jobs at the Dept. of Customs, Guyana Revenue Agency and the Mayor and City Council respectively. In consequence, Lieutenant Colonel Ulric Pilgrim was appointed to the position of Force Commander with the rank of full Colonel. With his appointment, the GDF now had a Force Commander, and a Chief of Staff. Lieutenant Colonel Vernon Williams was appointed Commanding Officer of the 1st Battalion, and Lieutenant Colonel Leonard B. Muss was appointed Commanding Officer of the 2nd Battalion. Major Carl Morgan was appointed second in command of the 1st Battalion, Major Desmond Roberts was appointed second in command of the 2nd Battalion.

In essence, politics was introduced into the Guyana Defence Force. Fundamentally, with this new era, many Education Officers were recruited into the Guyana Defence Force to teach political policies. These officers were Lieutenant Arlington Bancroft, Captain Leslie Robertson, Lieutenant Stephen Knights, Lieutenant Gladston Green and Major Gordon Daniels. A

Special Political Enumeration Council (SPEC) was formed by Major David Grainger in the Guyana Defence Force, and all the Officers were expected to join the group. They assembled for meetings at Congress Place in Camp Street. The word "Sir" was banned from the GDF and the word "Comrade" introduced. The Deputy Prime Minister Dr. Ptolemy Reid made the decision; that the Guyana Defence Force soldiers were not tough enough because we could not walk bare feet. The soldiers received the orders, that they should do their morning run barefooted. It was surprising to see the soldiers running through the streets of Georgetown barefooted; trying to evade broken bottles, bricks and other obstacles on the streets.

The year 1972 had a number of slogans. One of the slogans was "Advance Guyana." The GDF was required to clean the trenches around Georgetown. Prime Minister Forbes Burnham was pleased to see the soldiers in the Vlissengen Road canal; on his way from his home at Belfield to his office every day. I was sent with a Platoon of soldiers, to the West Coast to clean up the Magistrate Compound and the Police Compound at Vreedenhoop; as well as, trenches along the West Coast. We were supposed to be joined by members of the Peoples National Congress but none of them arrived to support us. Therefore, after two days that operation terminated.

The Prime Minister would bring the Peoples National Congress newspaper the "New Nation" every two weeks to the "Benab (hut)" in front of the GDF Compound. Officers met him there, and he gave us stacks of newspapers to be sold at the four city markets; Kitty, Bourda, Stabroek, and La Penitence. He would accompany us, and participated in selling the newspapers. One Officer, Captain Walter Spooner had left his bundle of newspapers under the Benab in defiance of his order. Shortly thereafter, he was no longer a member of the GDF.

Recruit Division and Training Wing.

In the month of March 1972, I was appointed Officer Commanding, the Recruit Division in the Training Corps. I trained my recruits at Base Tacama and every six weeks; at the conclusion of the training; I brought them out to Base Camp Ayanganna to be fitted for their uniforms; for the passing out parade. At the passing out parade, the Force Commander always took the salute; inspected the soldiers, and the training notes of his inspection would follow. I trained three intakes of recruits, between the period of March and December.

In January 1973 there were many changes in the Guyana Defence Force. The 1st Battalion was named Internal Operations Command and Lieutenant Colonel Carl Morgan was named Commanding Officer, Lieutenant Colonel Vernon Williams was transferred to the Engineers Battalion. The 2nd Battalion was named Border Operations Command and Lieutenant Colonel Leonard B. Muss was appointed Commanding Officer, and Major Desmond Roberts was appointed Director of the Guyana Youth Corps.

Moreover, in January 1973, I finished my last Recruit Course. Ensuingly, I was appointed Officer Commanding 3 Company. In view of that, I was authorized to wear the rank of Captain. I took over the Company from Captain Marcus Munroe, the Platoon Commanders in 3 Company were 2nd Lieutenant Neville Crawford, Gordon Cumberbatch, and Lennox De Cruz; my Company Sergeant Major was Warrant Officer Mohammed Yusuf, and my Colour Sergeant was Staff Sergeant Edward Washington. The Company was stationed at base Camp Ayanganna and normal military training was undertaken.

In March 1973, my Company won the first drill competition organized in the Guyana Defence Force for all Units of the GDF. The Force Commanded presented the Company with a trophy.

Shortly thereafter, the Company was posted to most border locations.

1973 General Elections

Also, in October of the same year, the Company was posted to Base Camp Stephenson. Afterwards, I was given specific orders, stating that for the impending general elections of the Country, I would be responsible for the Western Sector. The Western Sector; encompassed the West Bank Demerara, Canal No. 1 Polder, Canal No. 2 Polder, West Coast Demerara, East Bank Essequibo, Essequibo Islands, Essequibo Coast, and Bonasika. On October 25th, I moved my Company to West Coast Demerara and set up my headquarters at the Lenora Police Station; thus establishing a Joint Operation Centre.

Subsequently, I dispersed my Company at three locations. One Platoon commanded by 2nd Lieutenant Neville Crawford; were stationed at a government building at the Ministry of Works and Hydraulics compound at Vreed-en-hoop. 2 Platoon commanded by 2nd Lieutenant Lennox De Cruz; were stationed in a vacant fire station at Lenora. 3 Platoon, under the command of 2nd Lieutenants Gordon Cumberbatch and John Da Silva; were stationed at a government building at Vergenoegen Village. The Officer in charge of the West Demerara Police Division, Senior Superintendent Junior, gave me his personal residence at the rear of the Police Compound, for my accommodation.

The general elections were due to be held on November 7, 1973. I received my orders for the elections from Colonel Carl Morgan, Commanding Officer for Internal Operations Command, when we were aboard a Maritime Corps, Vosper patrol Boat at Vreed-en-hoop wharf. Simultaneously, he informed me that I was promoted to Substantive Rank of Captain. Specifically, my orders for the elections entailed picking up ballot boxes by air. There is a stretch of road on the West Coast Demerara highway; between the Boerasirie Bridge and the old Tuschen train station. This stretch of the highway was designated as an airstrip. The soldiers at Vergenoegen were ordered to make flambo lamps. They filled bottles with kerosene oil, and utilized jute bags/sacks to make strips as wicks (jute bags/sack are made from coarse fibre.)

On November 5, 1973, I relocated my headquarters from Lenora to the government building at Vergenoegen. Also on the same day, 2 Platoon Commanded by 2nd Lieutenant Lennox De Cruz was dispatched to the Essequibo Coast location. On the November 7th during the morning; the road blocks equipment were pre-positioned at the Boerasirie Bridge and the old Tuschen train station West Coast Demerara. The soldiers placed the flambo lamps, on both sides of the road between the Boerasirie Bridge and the old Tuschen train station. Also on the November 7, 2nd Lieutenant Neville Crawford and a section of soldiers were stationed at the Wales Police Station on West Bank Demerara. Their task was to escort the returning officers with their ballot boxes from West Bank Demerara, Canal No 1 Polder, Canal No 2 Polder, West Coast Demerara and East Bank Essequibo.

Precisely at 1800 hours on November 7, I left Parika wharf with a Section of soldiers on one of the three Vosper Patrol Boats (Jaguar, Ocelot & Morgay) acquired in 1969 from the UK, for the Essequibo Islands. We berthed at a wharf, at the back of Leguan Island and waited for the closing of the elections. At the close of the elections, the police at Leguan Island escorted the returning officers, with their ballot boxes to the Vosper Boat. The returning officers came aboard and we left for the Island of Wakenaam. When we arrived at Wakenaam, I went ashore with a section of soldiers, to escort the returning officers with their ballot boxes, because the local residents were preventing them from leaving the island. Afterwards, we left for Adventure Village on the Essequibo Coast.

At the location, 2nd Lieutenant Lennox De Cruz and the returning officers were waiting with their ballot boxes; his platoon of soldiers, were dispersed around the wharf. The elections officers with their ballot boxes boarded the boat, and then we left for Hogg Island. While there, we picked up one elections officer with his ballot box and we headed for Parika wharf. The Police at Bonasika escorted the elections officers and their ballot boxes from Bonasika to Parika wharf. I disembarked the boat at Parika; then one of my three ton trucks reversed onto the wharf. The returning officers with their ballot boxes boarded the vehicle. From there, we left for Tuschen train station; while we were there, a number of the Peoples Progressive Party supporters followed us in vehicles. They shouted that they were following us to Georgetown.

As a result, I radioed ahead to 2ndLieutenants Gordon Cumberbatch and John Da Silva, to be prepared to setup the roadblocks in position. When we reached, the old Tuschen train station the soldiers placed the roadblocks in position. Some of the soldiers stood guard at the roadblocks, while others ran down the road lighting the flambo lamps. The soldiers placed a lighted marker across the road by the Boraserie Bridge. Above us, a Guyana Airways Aircraft was circling; then began descending and landed on the temporary airstrip. The pilot of the aircraft was Captain Roland Da Silva. The returning officers then boarded the aircraft, with their ballot boxes and the aircraft left. The soldiers removed the roadblocks, to allow the flow of vehicular traffic to continue. That completed my tasks for the elections.

The next day on November 8, when I was at Lenora Police Station, I heard a news report that the Peoples National Congress had won the elections. Shortly thereafter, the Police reported to me, that a large crowd was approaching the police station to protest the results of the elections. Consequently, I went onto the public road with a section of soldiers and we form a line across the road. I stood in my land rover, and used my public address system to warn the crowd, I told them *"they were an unlawful assembly and they should disperse and it was their first and last warning."* The crowd started to disperse, some ran towards Stewartville and others ran into Lenora Village. That was the only incident I had during the elections. Unlike the situation on the Corentyne Coast, when Lieutenant Joseph Henry had to use maximum force, to secure the ballot boxes. The soldiers on the Corentyne Coast used live fire; to prevent persons from seizing the ballot boxes and two of them were killed. For the remainder of 1973, my Company executed operational duties in the Rupununi.

Chapter 11

Seconded to the Guyana National Service

On January 2nd, 1974, I was appointed Officer Commanding 2 Company at Base Timerhi. I took over the Company from Captain Robert Mitchell. The Officers under my command were 2nd Lieutenants Compton Ross, Charles Corlett, Joseph Martindale, and Kennard Ramphal and my Company Sergeant Major was Warrant Officer 2 Dennis Stewart. On January 15th, the Company left for Base Tacama to participate in the GDF jungle exercise. After we concluded the exercise, the Company left for Mabaruma Village (Barima-Waini.) On April 25th, it was published in the GDF Part 1 orders; that Captain Keith Ross was posted to the Guyana National Service. Captain Ross always advocated that he wanted to become the Deputy Director, of the Guyana Youth Corps before it became part of the Guyana National Service.

However, by that date he was an Administrative Staff Officer, in the office of the Chief of Staff, Brigadier General Clarence Price. The Chief of Staff had the orders changed, and Captain Ross's name was deleted from the orders. Hence, replacing it with my name, and I was posted to the Guyana National Service in May 1974. My first assignment was Staff Officer, at the Guyana National Service Secretariat in Georgetown. My main task, was to attest Guyana National Service personnel in Georgetown and swear them in; in the accordance with the "Defence Act 1501" so that they can have the same "Rights" as the GDF soldiers.

In October 1974, I was posted to Kimbia as the Training Officer. (Kimbia is located in the Ebini Savannhas of the Lower Berbice River) In February 1975, I was summoned, to the office of the Director General Norman McLean of the Guyana National Service. I received an on the spot promotion to the rank of Major. I was appointed the Centre Administrator at Papaya Training Centre. It was under construction at the time. (Papaya is located in the Barima-Waini of Region 1 in the North West District.)

Also in 1975, there were several changes in the Guyana Defence Force. The Internal Operations Command and Border Operations Command merged. Thus, the Infantry Brigade was established and Lieutenant Colonel Leonard B. Muss was appointed the Brigade Commander. 1, 2, and 3 Companies merged, and the Eleven Infantry Battalion was established. Major Robert Mitchell was appointed Battalion Commander, and the Battalion chose the Jaguar as their mascot. Therefore, the Battalion was called the Jaguar Battalion. The Battalion built a base at Low Creek on the Soesdyke Linden Highway, and the Base was called Camp Jagaurundi. Camp Jagaurundi became the Headquarters of Jaguar Battalion. 4, 5, and 6 Companies were merged; thereby, the Twelve Infantry Battalion was established. Major Marcus Munroe was appointed Commanding Officer of 12 Infantry Battalion. The Battalion chose the Parahna Fish as their mascot, so the Battalion was called the Perai Battalion. The Battalion Headquarters was based at Camp Stephenson at Timerhi. However, there was no accommodation for the Rifle Company at Camp Stephenson. Therefore, the Battalion built a base with several huts in the bushes at Timerhi; in the vicinity of

Red Water Creek. They were built with wood, canvas and zinc sheets. Their accommodations were not ideal, and this led to low morale in the Battalion.

Formation of a New Command

Further in March 1975, the Logistics Command was established; Major Rex Owen, the Finance Officer was appointed to Commanding Officer of the Logistics Command. The Logistics Command had the responsibility, of Finance and Logistics in the Guyana Defence Force. The Logistics Command had the responsibility, of Camp Stephenson. In June 1975, the Service Battalion was established, and Major Keith Ross was appointed Commanding Officer of the Service Battalion. The Service Battalion was based at Camp Stephenson. In October 1975, 2nd Lieutenants Andy Worrell, Joseph Harmon, and Edward Collins left Guyana for China to attend Military courses.

In January 1976, the Guyana Peoples Militia was formed and Lieutenant Colonel Cecil Martindale was recalled to the Guyana Defence Force. He was appointed Commandant of the Guyana Peoples Militia, with the Rank of Colonel and Senior Superintendent Wilfred Mentis, of the Guyana Police Force was appointed Administrative Staff Officer. The Guyana Defence Force posted a number of Officers, and Senior Ranks to the Guyana Peoples Militia as Staff and Training Officers. The Guyana Peoples Militia had a Company in all ten Regions of Guyana. The motto was "Every Citizen A Soldier". The Guyana Peoples Militia Headquarters was based at the Senior Staff Quarters at Diamond Estate on the East Bank Demerara.

Likewise, in 1976 all the members of the Reconnaissance Squadron, some members of 11 and 12 Infantry Battalions, the Mortar Company, and the Combat Engineers were sent to Cuba for military training. When these soldiers returned in June, all the members of the Reconnaissance Squadron were trained paratroopers. Captain Malcolm Williams was the Officer commanding the Reconnaissance Squadron. The Mortar Company was upgraded to the Artillery Battalion. The Battalion received a number of heavy weapons from the Democratic People's Republic of Korea. Major Ian Fraser was appointed the Battalion Commander. The Artillery Battalion was established and named their base Camp Groomes which was located at Sowyeo on the Soesdyke-Linden Highway. The camp was named after one of their soldiers who died in Cuba. They later upgraded the Artillery Battalion to the Support Weapons Battalion.

Return to the Guyana Defence Force

In June 1976, I returned to the Guyana Defence Force from the Guyana National Service, and I reported to Force Commander, Colonel Ulric Pilgrim. Subsequently, I was appointed the position of Base Commander at Camp Ayanganna. I was reverted to my Substantive Rank of Captain, since the GDF did not recognize Guyana National Service promotions. With this responsibility, I had at my disposal a staff car. It had a pennant that was used by the previous Base Commanders. As a result, it was the envy of most Senior Officers because they wanted the car. After serving as Base Commander for seven months, I was summoned to meet with the Force Commander. He informed me, that a number of senior officers had petitioned for the appointment of Base Commander. Since I was a "Middle Piece Officer" in the role of a senior officer, I was transferred to the Logistics Command as Deputy Battalion Commander in January 1977.

In 1976, the 13 Guard Battalion was established and Lieutenant Colonel Robert Mitchell was appointed Commanding Officer. The Battalion was based at Camp Stephenson. The13 Guard Battalion had the responsibility, of all the ceremonial parades and Guard of Honour in the Guyana Defence Force. Major Victor Wilson was appointed Commanding Officer of 11

Infantry Battalion. He took over command from Lieutenant Colonel Robert Mitchell. Major Randolph Johnson was appointed Commanding Officer of 12 Infantry Battalion. He took over command from Lieutenant Colonel Marcus Munroe. Consequently, Lieutenant Colonel Marcus Munroe was posted to Force Headquarters.

In December 1977, the Logistics Command was disbanded and Lieutenant Colonel Rex Owen, the Commanding Officer was appointed Quartermaster General (QMG) of the Guyana Defence Force. Furthermore, in December 1977 I was promoted to the rank of Major.

Appointed Second in Command to Training Corps

In January 1978, I was appointed Second in Command of the Training Corps. The Commanding Officer was Lieutenant Colonel Fairbairn Liverpool. My first assignment in January 1978 was President of the Court Martial of Captain Ronald Gajraj who was the paymaster. Captain Ronald Gajraj was accused of stealing, the soldiers' payroll money in the Training Corps. The Judge Advocate was Justice Sydney Miller. The trial lasted for two weeks and Captain Ronald Gajraj was found guilty and sentenced to two years imprisonment at the Georgetown Prison on Lot 12 Camp Street.

Captain Gajraj appealed his sentence, in the Supreme Court of Guyana and his conviction was overturned. Captain Gajraj was attending the University of Guyana at the time. He graduated with a law degree and practiced law. Later, Captain Gajraj returned to the Guyana Defence Force as a civilian lawyer and defended soldiers Pro -bono who were court martialled (Pro bono-for professional work undertaken voluntarily and without payment.)

School of Internal Security

In April 1978, the Guyana Defence Force established a school for Internal Security at the Maritime Corps location in Kingston, Georgetown. The School was named Internal Security School of Internal Security Studies "ISSISS." The School was given the Status of a Unit. Lieutenant Colonel Harry Hinds, Commanding Officer of the Maritime Corps was appointed Commanding Officer of the School. I was appointed Coordinator of the School. The school taught internal security duties to Officers of the Guyana Defence Force, Guyana Police Force and Guyana Fire Service. The curriculum comprised of lectures in Curfews, Cordon and Search, Road Blocks, Crowd Dispersal, Ambushes, Patrolling and other internal security duties. The duration of each course was for five weeks.

On the May 30th 1978, a second course commenced, and Lieutenant Colonel Fairbairn Liverpool was appointed Commanding Officer of the School. I continued as Coordinator of the school and taught most of the lectures to the students. The course concluded on June 15th. On July 1st, 1978 I was appointed Officer Commanding the Labaria Company. One hundred and twenty soldiers from the three Rifle Battalions were selected to form the Labaria Company. The Company participated in an Inter-Military Exchange Training Program with the British Army. Soldiers were selected every year to travel to England for training at various Military Schools. The Platoon Commanders were Second Lieutenants Roger Denny, Linden Ross, and Mark Rohlehr. Lieutenant Herbert Patterson was appointed Logistics Officer, and the Company Sergeant Major was Warrant Officer 2 Ronald Reynolds.

Further, in July 1978, Colonel Ulric Pilgrim, Commander of the GDF left for England, to attend the Defence College at Camberley, and Lieutenant Colonel Leonard B. Muss was appointed Commander of the GDF, with the rank of Colonel, and Lieutenant Colonel

Carl Morgan was appointed Brigade Commander. Colonel Muss served as Force Commander for a period of two months and then he resigned from the GDF. After the resignation of Colonel Muss, Lieutenant Colonel Morgan was appointed Force Commander with the rank of Colonel. Lieutenant Colonel Joseph Singh was then appointed Brigade Commander.

On October 1st, 1978 Lieutenant Colonel Fairbairn Liverpool and I, left for England to conduct a reconnaissance, of the Black Watch (Royal Highland) Regiment Base, at Catterick Garrison located in Richmondshire District of North Yorkshire, England. The reconnaissance visit was scheduled for two weeks.

For the duration of one week, while I was at Catterick Garrison, I wrote my syllabus for the training program. In addition, I identified the training equipment that I was required to utilize on the training. My next responsibility was to coordinate messing arrangements and organize accommodations for the Officers, Senior Ranks and other Ranks. In addition, I opened a bank account for the Company's financial transactions.

Chapter 12

Appointed Commanding Officer of Training Corps

Two weeks later, Lieutenant Colonel Fairbairn Liverpool and I returned to Guyana from England. Shortly after our return, Lieutenant Colonel Liverpool was selected to attend the University of Guyana, and I was appointed Commanding Officer of Training Corps at Base Timerhi.

Joint Guyana Defence Force and United Kingdom

Inter-Military Exchange Program

In November 1978, a company of soldiers from the Black Watch (Royal Highland) Regiment arrived in Guyana. The Officer in command was Major De Berg Ferguson; who I had met in England ten years earlier, when I attended the Senior Non-Commissioned Officers Weapons and Tactics Course, at the School of Infantry at Brecon in South Wales Great Britain. We renewed our acquaintances; I handed over my living quarters to him at the Officers Mess at Camp Stephenson, Timerhi. Two days later, I left Guyana for England, with a Company of one hundred and thirty soldiers on the Inter-Military exchange program. Ten of the soldiers, who travelled with us, were not members of my Company, they were Officers and Senior Ranks sent to England on various assignments.

We attended the five weeks training program, at the Black Watch (Royal Highland) Regiment Base at Catterick Garrison. Our program entailed training at the Electrical Rifle Ranges; participating in joint exercises with the Black Watch Regiment, in Army Personnel Carriers (APCs) and Battle Tanks. At the conclusion, of the training, we visited the City of London and historical places. They were the London Bridge, Buckingham Palace, the House of Commons, Stonehenge, and a two days visit to Scotland. After the tour, the Company left Scotland by bus to Heathrow Airport for a flight to return to Guyana. I remained in England for two weeks. In December of the same year, Colonel Ulric Pilgrim returned to Guyana from Defence College in England. Subsequently, he resumed command of the Guyana Defence Force (GDF).

Jonestown Massacre

During this period, the Jonestown incident occurred in the North West District of Guyana on November 18, 1978, where more than 900 Americans living there; who had relocated from San Francisco, California, drank a toxic mix of Kool-Aid and cyanide, on the orders from their leader Jim Jones. Congressman Leo Ryan, who initially was concerned, about the welfare of the people decided to travel to Jonestown on a fact-finding mission. Along with him were three journalists - San Francisco Examiner photographer Greg Robinson, NBC correspondent Don Harris, and NBC photographer Bob Brown. While standing at a nearby airfield, they along with a People Temple member, Patricia Parks, were all shot and killed.

To investigate the massacre, Major Randolph Johnson, and the soldiers of Perai Battalion left Base Timerhi, for Matthews Ridge in a Guyana Airways Dakota (DC-3/ C-47) aircraft. They landed at Matthews Ridge airstrip at night, where they rested at the Guyana Defence Force (GDF) Outpost near the airstrip. The next day, the soldiers left Matthews Ridge by train for Port Kaituma. Major Johnson, Lieutenant Colonel Gregory Gaskin and a representative of the Peoples Temple office, from Georgetown flew over Jonestown; in a GDF helicopter piloted by Major Larry London. On their way to Port Kaituma, they were flying at low altitude, and observed bodies of members of the Peoples Temple lying on the ground. The helicopter landed at Port Kaituma, and Major Johnson re-joined his men and led them into Jonestown.

The Combat Team Commanders Course in the United Kingdom

On January 2nd, 1979, I attended the Combat Team Commanders Course in England, at the School of Infantry at Warminster, UK. The duration of the course lasted for six weeks. On February 20th, 1979, I returned to Guyana, and I was appointed the Base Commander of Camp Stephenson. Also in February 1979, Colonel Pilgrim wrote a letter to Prime Minister Burnham requesting to be appointed the Chief of Staff of The Guyana Defence Force. It was the second letter on this matter that Colonel Pilgrim had sent to Prime Minister Burnham. In the letter it was stated that if his request to be appointed the Chief of Staff is not granted; then he should be allowed to attend the University of Guyana as a fulltime student. Colonel Pilgrim had taken a chance in writing the letters, because he felt that he was the only Officer, in the Guyana Defence Force with the applicable training to be appointed to the position of Chief of Staff. Prime Minister Burnham summoned Colonel Pilgrim to his office; counselled him on his letter and told him to go and attend the University of Guyana.

Appointment of the New Chief-of-Staff (COS)

In July 1979, Prime Minister Burnham then ordered the Chief of Staff, Brigadier Clarence Price to retire from the Guyana Defence Force because he was two years above the age limit for serving officers. While Officers in the Guyana Defence Force were waiting to be appointed Chief of Staff and Force Commander; President Burnham appointed the Director General of The Guyana National Service, Norman McLean the Chief of Staff with the rank of Brigadier. Colonel Carl Morgan was appointed Chief Administrator of Matarkai Garrison, Lieutenant Colonel David Grainger, was appointed Force Commander with the rank of Colonel. Lieutenant Colonel Joseph Singh continued as a Brigade Commander.

Appointed Commanding Officer
12th Infantry Battalion

The Twelve Infantry Battalion (Perai) was known as the worst Battalion in the Guyana Defence Force (GDF). Prime Minister Burnham wanted to send Colonel Desmond Roberts, from the Guyana National Service, to take over command of the Battalion. However, Colonel Roberts was able to convince Prime Minister Burnham, that Colonels do not command Battalions in the GDF. Therefore, Colonel Roberts was not assigned to command the Twelve Infantry Battalion (Perai). When Brigadier Norman McLean assumed his position, as the Chief of Staff of the Guyana Defence Force, he was able to acquire a number of buildings, at Long Creek on the Soesdyke-Linden Highway. These buildings formerly housed re-migrating Guyanese, who had lived there for a number of years, before being allocated the farmlands on the Soesdyke-Linden Highway. The Twelve Infantry Battalion; was removed from their location at Timerhi to Long Creek. Thus, Long Creek became the Base of Twelve Infantry Battalion (Perai). In July 1979, I was appointed Commanding Officer of Twelve Infantry Battalion.

I took over the Battalion from Major Randolph Johnson. The Officers under Command were Captain Edward Collins, Officer Commanding 4 Company, Captain Chabilall Ramsroop, Officer Commanding 5 Company, Captain Lennox Luncheon, Officer Commanding 6 Company, Captain Leslie Green, Officer Commanding Headquarters Company, and my Adjutant was Lieutenant Patrick Stevens. My Regimental Sergeant Major was Warrant Officer 1 Ulric Sutton, and my Regimental Quartermaster Sergeant was Sergeant Aubrey Layne. There were eight buildings at Long Creek, one building was identified as a Headquarters Building, another building was identified as an Ordnance Ration Store, two Dormitories were identified as accommodations for other ranks, and four three bedrooms buildings were identified as accommodations for officers and senior ranks.

The Battalion had its own carpenters and masons; but with the help of the Engineers Command, we started renovations of the buildings at Long Creek. The soldiers repaired and painted the headquarters building. Consequently, it was converted into the Battalion Headquarters. We build a large arms store, and divided it into four individual arms stores for the four Companies. We repaired and painted the Ordinance and Ration stores. We build a kitchen mess hall Complex; an all ranks club, a barbershop, and finally we fenced the camp. We pumped water from Long Creek, to an overhead tank for the camp water supply. We cleared lands, adjacent to the Base for a parade square; painted and repaired the two dormitories, and the four accommodations for officers and senior ranks. In actual fact, this completed our renovations, and established the Long Creek Base. These new accommodations, improved the morale among the soldiers. Subsequently, I posted twenty long absentees (AWOL) soldiers to the GDF Headquarters, for the removal of their names from the Battalion roll.

I took, the Battalion to Tacama Battle School, for two weeks of intensive training in minor field tactics. Once, the training concluded, we returned to Base Long Creek. Subsequently, the Battalion was posted to various Cuyuni River locations. For the remainder of the year, we carried out our border commitments in the Cuyuni, Eterinbang, Kaikan, Paruima and Kamarang. As well as, Lethem in the Rupununi that was added to the responsibilities of the Battalion.

Joint GDF and UK Exchange Military Training

In November 1979, a Company from the Kings Regiment of the British Army arrived in Guyana for the Inter-Military Exchange Training Program. Simultaneously, Major Perry Foo took the Labaria Company to England for the exchange visit. My Battalion, carried out joint training exercises with a Company of British soldiers, on the back lands of the Soesdyke-Linden Highway; to as far as Mahaica Creek. On December 10th 1979, the Labaria Company returned from England; then the British soldiers from the Kings Regiment departed for England. Shortly after his return, Major Perry Foo was appointed Second in Command of 12 Infantry Battalion. He brought twelve football jerseys for the football team from England and presented them to the Battalion.

The Chief of Staff, Brigadier General Norman McLean was building his ranch on the Soesdyke-Linden Highway. Every time he visited his ranch, he drove into the Base at Long Creek without prior notification. Customarily, I met with him, and escorted him around the Base for an inspection. Afterwards, he would leave and continue the journey to his ranch.

Furthermore, in January 1980, Warrant Office 1 Joseph Glasgow was appointed Regimental Sargent Major of 12 Infantry Battalion replacing Warrant Officer 1 Ulric Sutton.

In February 1980, Major Foo my Second in Command was posted to the Guyana Peoples Militia as a Staff Officer. Further, my Battalion was re-posted to our border locations and carried out operational duties in the Cuyuni River area and at Lethem in the Rupununi until July the same year.

Also, in the month of July, the Guyana Defence Force (GDF) established a competition to select the best Unit or Battalion in the GDF. Participating in the competition were 11 Infantry Battalion, 12 Infantry Battalion, 13 Guards Battalion, the Support Weapons Battalion, the two Bases Camp Ayanganna, and Camp Stephenson, the Maritime Corps, and Training Corps. Each Unit or Battalion were represented by a Company of no less than 50 soldiers. 12 Infantry Battalion was represented by 4 Company, Commanded by Captain Edward

Collins. The competition commenced on August 1st, with a run and shoot, that started from the junction of the Soesdyke-Linden Highway to Timerhi Rifle Ranges, a distance of six miles.

On the day of the competition, 4 Company left the Base at Long Creek in two 3 ton vehicles for the junction of Soesdyke-Linden Highway. On our way one of the vehicles broke down with engine problems; therefore, I radioed the Brigade Commander, Lieutenant Joseph Singh and informed him of the situation. He indicated that he would wait for us. After repairing the vehicle, we then continued on our journey to the starting point, at the junction of Soesdyke-Linden Highway. We arrived approximately fifteen minutes late. As a consequence, the Brigade Commander penalized the Battalion fifty points, a decision that was ordained so that the battalion could not win the competition.

However, by the end of the days' competitions that involved several events at Timerhi Rifle ranges; 4 Company had not only erased the deficit of fifty points, but led the competition in many events. After five days of intense competition; in all aspects of military activities, the competition concluded with a swimming event; that was held at Camp Stephenson swimming pool. At the conclusion of all the events, 4 Company was declared the winners of the competition. As a result, 12 Infantry Battalion (Perai) was recognized as the champion Battalion. For its victories, the status of 12 Infantry Battalion, was elevated from the worst Battalion to the best Battalion in the Guyana Defence Force (GDF). As a reward, for winning the competition 4 Company was selected, to go to England for the next Inter-Military Exchange Program.

Leguan Island - Fiasco

On August 15th Deputy Commissioner of Police Cecil (Skip) Roberts made a request to the Chief of Staff, Brigadier Norman McLean for a number of soldiers to accompany his detectives on an operation on the Island of Leguan. The Chief of Staff, Brigadier General McLean, passed on the orders directly to me, to provide a Platoon to accompany the detectives. 1 Platoon of 4 Company, Commanded by 2nd Lieutenant Mark O'Lear, was ordered to accompany the detectives the following day on August 16th. However, when the Brigade Commander, Joseph Singh was informed of the operation, he summoned me to his office to let me know that he was aware of the operation. He requested an aircraft from the Air Corps and a photographer. Then the three of us went flying over the Island of Leguan several times, taking pictures of all the buildings on the Island. We took pictures from over the Atlantic Ocean of the Island, and over the Essequibo River of the Island.

Later that day I was summoned to Guyana Defence Force Headquarters operations room, for orders by the Brigade Commander, Joseph Singh. He had all the pictures pasted unto a wall. He reiterated the orders, for the operation that I had already received previously from the Chief of Staff, Brigadier McLean. Shortly after the Deputy Commissioner of Police Cecil (Skip) Roberts telephoned the Chief of Staff, Brigadier General McLean to inform him that the Brigade Commander, Joseph Singh had jeopardized the operation by flying over the Island several times. The Brigade Commander, Joseph Singh quickly took down the pictures from the wall that were taken from over the Island, and left those that were taken from over the Atlantic Ocean and the Essequibo River.

When he was questioned by the Chief of Staff, Brigadier General McLean, with respect to why he had flown over the Island of Leguan, the Brigade Commander, Joseph Singh said "he never flew over the Island of Leguan and that the Chief of Staff could ask me." I remained quiet and did not respond because I knew that the Brigade Commander, Joseph Singh had misled the Chief of Staff, Brigadier General McLean about the situation. The next day, Lieutenant Rohlehr and his Platoon accompanied the detectives from the Criminal Investigations Department (CID) to the Island of Leguan. When they arrived there, all the persons that they wanted to arrest had fled the Island.

Chapter 13

Guyana's First Executive President.

Linden Forbes Sampson Burnham, O.E., S.C.
Prime Minister of Guyana, 1964-1980

President of the Cooperative
Republic of Guyana, 1980-1985

Courtesy of Mrs. Roxane Burnham-Van West Charles

On October 6, 1980, with the proclamation of the New Constitution, Prime Minister Linden Forbes S. Burnham became

Guyana's first Executive President, a position he held until his death in 1985.

The general elections were due to be held in November 1980. The British Government did not send the British troops to Guyana, to participate in the Inter-Military Exchange Training Program. It was allegedly stated, that Prime Minister Margaret Thatcher, did not want it to appear that she was sending troops in support of President Burnham during the elections. As a result, of Prime Minister Margaret Thatcher's decision, President Burnham terminated the program that was scheduled in November and it ceased to exist.

The Battalion was given the Western Sector, the same sector that I was responsible for, when I was a Company Commander in 1973. The Western Sector was West Bank Demerara, Numbers One and Two Canal Polder, West Coast Demerara, East Bank Essequibo, Essequibo Islands, Essequibo Coast and Bonasika Village on the Essequibo River. Prior to the general elections, 5 Company, Commanded by Captain Chabilall Ramsaroop was dispatched to the Essequibo Coast. When he was there, they established a Base at Anna Regina, Police Station. The remainder of the Battalion was stationed at Lenora Police Station on West Coast Demerara.

For this general elections the Guyana Defence Force soldiers were not required, to escort the returning officers with their ballot boxes, because, the counting of the votes were done at all the polling stations. We were only required to patrol the polling areas, to ensure that the elections were free of trouble. The Peoples National Congress won the general elections. After the elections, 5 Company was ordered to remain on the Essequibo Coast. During this time, there were a series of motor vehicle accidents that involved Battalions' vehicles on the Essequibo Coast.

As a consequence, I visited Captain Ramsaroop, to investigate the accidents that involved these vehicles, and secured copies of the police report. I perused the reports, and afterwards, submitted them to the Chief of Staff (COS), Brigadier General McLean. The Battalion vehicles were also involved in many accidents on the East Bank Demerara. One vehicle ran off the road damaging the bridge of a shop. The COS counselled me about these accidents because I was ultimately responsible for the vehicles in the Battalion.

On January 5th, 1981 the Battalion was in training, on a classification rifle shoot on the Timerhi Rifle Ranges. Captain Lester Green was left in charge of security, for the Base at Long Creek. The Chief of Staff Brigadier General McLean, in one of his usual impromptu visits to the Base; was met by Captain Green. Because he was not wearing a head dress; he did not salute the COS. Immediately, thereafter the Chief of Staff saw Lieutenant Patrick Stephens, Adjutant of the Battalion and summoned him. Lieutenant Stephens started walking towards the Chief of Staff when he was ordered to move in double time. Lieutenant Stephens did not comply with his order; because no self-respecting Officer would have done so. The Chief of Staff became angry and immediately summoned me from Timerhi Rifle Ranges. However, when I arrived at the Base, he had already left for his ranch. I remained at the Base, for approximately two hours until he returned. On his arrival at the Base, he reported the conduct of Captain Green and Lieutenant Stephens to me. Further, he informed me to submit written reports of the incidents. Ultimately, these incidents resulted in disciplinary actions against both Officers.

At the end of January 1981, it was posted in Guyana Defence Force orders, that I was transferred to the Training Corps and appointed Office Commanding the Tactics Division. Consequently, Major Michael Atherly was appointed Commanding Officer of 12 Infantry Battalion. On being posted to Training Corps I immediately requested to attend the University of Guyana. Lieutenant Colonel Alan Lewis and I were selected. Subsequently, it was published in the Guyana Defence Force orders that we would attend the University of Guyana.

However, Major George Maynard a staff officer of Guyana Defence Force Headquarters, and Major Larry London the Commanding Officer of the Air Corps also requested to attend the University of Guyana. Since, they could not send four of us, Lieutenant Colonel Alan Lewis and my name were deleted from the orders; thereby inserting Major Maynard and Major London names to attend the University of Guyana.

In the month of April 1981, Lieutenant Colonel Watson Joseph, Commanding Officer of the Training Corps, resigned from the Guyana Defence Force and I was appointed Commanding Officer of Training Corps.

Chapter 14

Joint Services Presentation on Defence of Guyana

In the month of May, there was a presentation held by the Joint Services on the defence of Guyana for President Burnham. The presentation took place in the Lecture Hall at Camp Ayanganna. Brigadier David Granger did the presentation on the defence of Guyana, for the Guyana Defence Force. When it was time for the Guyana National Service presentation, the Deputy Director General Charwin Burnham got up to make the presentation. At that time, President Burnham enquired, where the Director General, Colonel Desmond Roberts was. He was informed that Colonel Roberts was on leave. President Burnham wanted to know how Colonel Desmond Roberts was on leave, and he who is the President was present at the conference. President Burnham said "he did not want to hear the presentation from Deputy Director General Charwin Burnham." However, for the afternoon session, Director General Colonel Roberts arrived and conducted the National Service Presentation. Further, Major Perry Foo did the presentation for the Guyana Peoples Militia. The Commandant for the Guyana Peoples Militia, Colonel Cecil Martindale did not attend the presentation.

On May 30th 1981, Colonel Roberts Director General of the Guyana National Service and Colonel Martindale Commandant of the Guyana Peoples Militia, were appointed Military Attaches to Brazil and Venezuela respectively. Lieutenant Colonel Joseph Singh was appointed Director General of the Guyana National Service, with the rank of Colonel. Colonel Carl Morgan was appointed Commandant of the Guyana Peoples Militia. Colonel Roberts and Colonel Martindale never took up the two appointments in Brazil or Venezuela. The Government stated that it did not have the necessary funds, to establish those two positions in Brazil and Venezuela. Consequently, Colonel Roberts and Colonel Martindale were both posted to Defence Headquarters as Staff Officers.

In the month of June 1981, I was summoned by the Chief of Staff, Brigadier General McLean and the Force Commander to report at Defence Headquarters. At that time, I was told that I was selected to attend the Canadian Land Forces Command and Staff College in Canada. In accordance with their orders, I left Guyana on August 1st 1981, to attend the Canadian Land Forces Staff School, and Staff College. The Canadian Land Forces Staff School was located on Avenue Road in Toronto, Ontario. The courses commenced in August and concluded in October. At the end of October, I attended the Canadian Land Forces Staff College in Kingston, Ontario. The course was concluded in June 1982 and I returned to Guyana in Mid-June 1982.

Commander of Special Forces

On my return to Guyana, I was summoned to attend a meeting with the Chief of Staff Brigadier General McLean and Force Commander Brigadier David Granger. The Chief of Staff, Brigadier General McLean read my report from the Canadian Land Forces Staff College to me. In actual fact, after he read the report to me, I was appointed Commanding Officer Designate of

3 Special Force Battalion. After being appointed Commanding Officer, I formed the new 3 Special Force Battalion.

The Battalion was comprised of the Reconnaissance Squadron, Commanded by Captain Walter Sargent. The Reconnaissance Squadron was later renamed the Airborne Company, the Jungle Company Commanded by Captain Dot Hemraj; and the Maritime Raiders Commanded by Captain Montage Congraves. My Adjutant was Captain Randolph Storm, and my Regimental Sergeant Major (RSM) was Warrant Officer 1 Rocky Mohamed. The uniform of the Special Force Battalion was a camouflage suit; the Battalion was based at Camp Stephenson. The Battalion carried out a number of clandestine operations with the Guyana Police Force. The operations were conducted at Black Bush Polder, the Corentyne Coast, Ituni on the Lower Berbice River, the backlands of Soesdyke-Linden Highway, and at Port Kaituma Region Number One. Those operations were executed by the Jungle Company. Similarly, we conducted operations at Makouria on the Essequibo River, at St. Marys Village and Charity Village on the Pomeroon River. Those operations were executed by the Maritime Raiders.

Likewise, the Airborne Company carried out a number of parachutes jumps that were executed at Base Timerhi, for the Chief of Staff Brigadier General McLean and other Senior Officers. Similarly, at the Tacama Battle School, President L.F.S. Burnham witnessed the Support Weapons Battalion carried out a number of demonstrations of heavy weapons by the Artillery Battalion. In addition, members of the Airborne Company conducted a parachute jump. At the conclusion of the events, members of the Airborne Company conducted a jump over the Atlantic Ocean into Camp Ayanganna for members of the Defence Force.

Also, in November at the conclusion of the Guyana Defence Force exercises in the Ebini Savannah; the Airborne Company executed parachutes jumps at the finale of the exercise. During the parachutes jumps, Private Harry Kissoon exited the aircraft but his parachute did not deploy. As a consequence, he plummeted to the ground and was killed in front of thousands of Guyana Defence Force soldiers. Private Kissoon was the last soldier executing the parachute jumps on that day. Regrettably, I left Ebini to convey the news of his death to his parents who lived at Burma on the East Coast Demerara. After informing his parents of the accident, I left for the Battalion Headquarters at Base Timerhi. One week later, I returned to Burma with soldiers for his military funeral. After the funeral service he was cremated at Mahaicony Foreshore.

Relocation of Flag Raising Ceremony

In 1983 President Linden Forbes S. Burnham, moved the Flag Raising Ceremony of the Mashramani celebrations from the National Park on Thomas Lands, Georgetown to The Square of The Revolution, where a Cuffy Monument is erected on Vlissingen Road. On February 22nd, 1983 at 2359 hours, 3 Guards Battalion performed the first Guard of Honour for President Burnham, at The Square of The Revolution. On February 23rd 1983, there was a parade around Georgetown by the Joint Services; comprised of Guyana Defence Force (GDF) Guyana National Service (GNS) Guyana Peoples Militia (GPM) and the Guyana Police Force (GPF). The parade was led by 13 Guards Battalion; the parade Commander was Major Hilton Mc David. The parade marched pass President Burnham at The Square of The Revolution. During the parade, it was reported that 13 Guards Battalion marched pass President Burnham out of step with the music of the band. Immediately, after the parade, the President as Commander in Chief, ordered 13 Guards Battalion to do exit drills, on the parade square at Camp Ayanganna. Afterwards, President Burnham visited Camp Ayanganna, to observe them being drilled by Warrant Officer 1 Ulric Sutton, the Force Regimental Sargent Major.

On February 24, 1983, I was summoned to Defence Headquarters by the Chief of Staff, Major General Norman MacLean and the Force Commander, Brigadier General David Granger. At the meeting, I was given the order to take over 13 Guards Battalion as Commanding Officer, to save the Guyana Defence Force from further embarrassment. In the month of March 1983, I handed over 3 Special Force Battalion to Major Michael Atherly and took over the command of 13 Guards Battalion from Major Hilton Mc David.

In my role as Commander, I carried out intensive training; in arms and foot drills with the Battalion. In June 1983, there was the annual drill competition for all the units in the Guyana Defence Force (GDF). As a result of 13 Guards Battalion excellent drills performance, I won my second drill competition in the Guyana Defence Force (GDF) with the Battalion. The 13 Guards Battalion provided all Guards of Honour for President Burnham when he was leaving Guyana; on his return to Guyana, and for the sessions at the opening of Parliament. On November 1, 1983 I was promoted to the rank of Lieutenant Colonel. On November 11, 1983 I commanded the Remembrance Day Parade at the Cenotaph in Main Street, Georgetown.

In February 1984, I commanded the parade of the Joint Services. The parade marched pass President Burnham at The Square of The Revolution. This time, the result was different; they were cheers instead of jeers. The Battalion continued to carry out Guard of Honours for President Burnham when he is leaving Guyana; on his return to Guyana, Guard of Honour for visiting Heads of State and Guard of Honour at the sessions for the opening of Parliament.

In the month of May 1984, I was appointed Aide-de-camp (ADC) to the Chairman of the Collective Presidency of Yugoslavia, Mika Spiljak on his state visit to Guyana.

Overseas Visits to Bulgaria, Ukraine and China

In the month of September 1984, I was appointed Aide-de-camp (ADC) to President Burnham for his State visits to Bulgaria, The Ukraine and China. As a result, of my appointment Major Webbna Cambridge was appointed Acting Commanding Officer of 13 Guards Battalion. I took up my appointment at the Presidential Secretariat on Vlissingen Road. My office was situated next to President Burnham's office.

President Burnham, his wife Viola, a small party of dignitaries, and I, left Guyana on October 15, 1984. We departed in President Burnham's Turbo Prop aircraft for Trinidad. It was our first stop of the State visits to Bulgaria, Ukraine, and China. In addition, there was a thirty-five members delegation with us; they travelled by Guyana Airways Hawker Siddeley aircraft to Trinidad. On our arrival at Piarco Airport, Trinidad; we were met by Prime Minister George Chambers of Trinidad and Tobago. The delegation had lunch with Prime Minister Chambers at Piarco airport. On the tarmac of the airport, there was a beaming white Russian twin engine jet aircraft painted in Guyana colours. The first class compartment, of the aircraft was converted into two bedrooms, for President Burnham and his wife Viola. The same afternoon, the delegation boarded the aircraft, and we departed for England.

On our arrival in England, we disembarked at Heathrow airport, and were welcomed by members of the Guyana Mission in Great Britain. While we were there, President Burnham, and his wife Viola left for London. They returned to the aircraft approximately three hours later. They boarded the aircraft, and we left for Shannon Airport in Ireland where the aircraft was refueled.

After, refueling the aircraft, we left for a five day State visit to Bulgaria. On our arrival in Bulgaria we were welcomed at the airport by officials of the Bulgarian Government. We left the airport and travelled to the Bulgarian Capital City Sofia. Later that evening, we had one official meeting with the President of Bulgaria and other Government officials of Bulgaria. Once the meeting concluded, we had a State Dinner. The following day we commenced our scheduled visits. We visited several historical places during our five day visits there. One of the places that we visited was The Georgi Dimitrov Mausoleum in Sofia, Bulgaria. Georgi Dimitrov, was a former Bulgarian President, and the Mausoleum was built in 1949 for his body after his death. We concluded the five days by spending a day at the Black Sea Resort.

The next day we left for a two day visit to the Ukraine. On our arrival at the Boryspil International Airport in Kiev, we were met by officials of The Ukraine Government. From the airport, we travelled to The Ukraine Capital City, Kiev. During the evening we had dinner with President Mykola Andriyovych Livytsky of the People's Republic of Ukraine and other Government officials.

The ensuing day, we took two buses and went on sightseeing tours of The Ukraine Capital, Kiev. The sightseeing tours were the conclusion of our two day visit in The Ukraine. Before we left for the airport for our trip to China, we were delayed by the Ukrainian Secret Service. Apparently, they thought that we were leaving one person behind. After checking the passports, and the manifest of the aircraft, they determined that all the members of the delegation were onboard the aircraft; therefore, we were allowed to depart.

On our arrival in China, the aircraft landed at Tiananmen Square. When we disembarked, there was a Guard of Honour provided by the Peoples' Liberation Army. Members of the Guard of Honour were no less than six feet four inches in height. President Burnham and I inspected the Guard of Honour. It ended with a run pass by the Guard of Honour; a Chinese custom. We had two meetings during the day, with Leader Deng Xiaoping and Premier Zhao Ziyang in the Great Hall of China. The first evening, the Chinese Government hosted the dinner. On the second evening, the Guyanese delegation hosted the dinner in the Great Hall of China. We visited several historical places, including the Great Wall of China. President L.F.S. Burnham and I did not visit the Great Wall, because he had seen the Great Wall before on a previous visit. I stayed with him in the Presidential bungalow. While we were alone together, we got more acquainted with each other.

After visiting in Beijing for five days, we left for a two day visit to Chengdu in Southwest China. Chengdu is the home of the Giant Pandas, and also the Panda zoo. The delegation visited the Panda zoo and other historical places in Chengdu. At the conclusion, of the two days visit to Chengdu, there was a cultural presentation by the Chinese troops. After, the presentation, the delegation left China and returned to Guyana on October 30th 1984. On our arrival at Timerhi International Airport, we were welcomed by a Guard of Honour, Vice-President Desmond Hoyte and other Government officials. President Burnham inspected the Guard of Honour, Commanded by Major Weddna Cambridge. On my return to Georgetown, I spent one week at the Presidential Secretariat. In a private meeting with President Burnham, he told me that I would accompany him to Japan in 1985 on his next State visit. After I left the Secretariat, I returned to 13 Guards Battalion and took Command of the Battalion.

Death of President Linden Forbes Sampson Burnham

February 20, 1923 - August 6, 1985

In August 1985, while waiting for the State visit to Japan, President Burnham entered the Georgetown Public Hospital on May 19th for a minor operation; it was something that he would not have ordinarily done. During the surgery, it was reported that President Burnham heart had stopped. His heart machine was left in his residence at Belfield. Apparently, the Hospital was not equipped with one at the time. The helicopter was dispatched back to his residence for the heart machine. While it was en-route to his home President Burnham died. Guyana's first Executive President, Linden Forbes Sampson Burnham died on the operating table.

I commanded President Burnham's first funeral parade from the National Park on Thomas Road to the Seven Ponds Monument in the Georgetown Botanical Gardens; where the President body was entombed. That night President Burnham's body was removed from the tomb and taken to Merriman Funeral Home, at 55 Lime and Bent Streets, Werk-en-Rust, Georgetown, then to Cuba, and from there it was taken to Russia.

The plan was for President Burnham's body to be mummified, then, build a Mausoleum in the Georgetown Botanical Gardens for his body. Guyana being a tropical Country; a Mausoleum would require a temperate climate. Essentially, it would have been necessary to build an ice house in the Botanical Gardens, and a power plant to supply electricity to the ice house. Conversely, since those aspects rendered it inconceivable, for them to build that precise type of Mausoleum, the plan was rescinded. Accordingly, President Burnham's body was returned to Guyana from Russia. I commanded President Burnham's second funeral parade from the National Cultural Centre,

Georgetown to his tomb in the Botanical Gardens. His body was entombed there as his final resting place.

In 1986, the Burnham Mausoleum was finally erected at the Seven Ponds Monument in the Botanical Gardens for the entombed body of President Linden Forbes Sampson Burnham.

With the death of Guyana's first Executive President Linden Forbes Sampson Burnham, Vice President Desmond Hoyte was appointed President of Guyana. In October 1985, on his first visit to the Guyana Defence Force Officers conference, President Hoyte told the Guyana Defence Force Officers the Guyana Defence Force was too big, and that he wanted an affordable Army. As a consequence, they had to reduce the size of the Guyana Defence Force.

The 13 Guards Battalion, that I commanded and the last Battalion that was established, in the Guyana Defence Force was the first Battalion to be disbanded. I was appointed Deputy Commander of the Ground Forces Group. The Ground Forces Group had replaced the Infantry Brigade. The Commander of the Ground Forces Group was Colonel Robert Mitchell. As Deputy Commander of the Ground Forces Group, I was given special responsibility for all the Border Locations.

Chapter 15

Matarkai Garrison – North West District (Region 1)

The name Matarkai is the abbreviation for Matthews Ridge, Arakaka, and Kaituma.

In early 1952, Manganese Mines Management, Ltd; a subsidiary of Union Carbide Corporation of New York applied for a lease in Matthews Ridge (North-West District / Region 1) to mine extensive deposits of manganese ore. The production of columbite - tantalite on a small scale was begun in 1952. Between1961-1966, over 1.7million metric tons of 40%+ Manganese (Mn) concentrate was produced.

The persistent, sabre rattling by Venezuela resumed; immediately after Guyana's independence on May 26, 1966. Union Carbide Corporation which had operations in the Venezuela-Guyana Shield became 'risk averse' (an investor who, when faced with two investments with a similar expected return [but different risks], will prefer the one with the lower risk), prompting them to abandon their operations in Guyana, leaving among other property holdings, heavy equipment, railroad locomotives, river punts and a 22 mile / 35 Km railroad that ran between Matthews Ridge and Port Kaituma.

The Venezuela Guyana shield is the northern part of the Amazonian craton in South America and includes parts of Venezuela, Colombia, Guyana, Brazil, Suriname, and French Guiana.

In1966, Union Carbine of the United States, the owners of the African Manganese Company, at Matthews Ridge in the North West Region (Barima-waini) of Guyana, ceased their operations. The company was closed and sold to the Government of Guyana for one dollar. Consequently, they departed from Guyana. Although the Government of Guyana had the opportunity to mine the manganese; they did not have the ships to transport the manganese ore for sale on the International market. Consequently, the Government decided to change the former manganese complex into an agricultural project. An Agricultural School was established at Arakaka on the Barima River. They named the school Burnham Agricultural Institute (BAI) and the Principal was Mr. Edmund Dawes. The name of the project was Matarkai.

The first Chief Administrator of Matarkai Agriculture Project was Mr. Lewis Amsterdam. The agricultural project planted Irish potatoes, cassava (yuca), turmeric, pineapples, oranges, lemons, and grass for the herd of cattle that Matarkai owned. The agricultural project, established two modern cassava mills; one at Matthews Ridge and the other at Port Kaituma. The project was financed with millions of dollars most of which was used to pay the former workers of the manganese mine for becoming farmers in the agricultural project.

In 1970, the Guyana Defence Force (GDF) posted 4 Company to Matarkai. The Company took up residence at The Ridge on Hill Two. Additionally, they established an outpost at Matthews Ridge Airport; on a hill above the Airport Building.

Evidently by 1978, the agriculture project had failed, from lack of production in commercial quantities and the high cost of transporting produce to the coastal areas including the urban center, Georgetown. At that stage, the Government decided, to hand over the administration of Matarkai to the GDF. The name of Matarkai Agriculture Project; changed under the GDF. The new name was Matarkai Garrison. The first military Chief Administrator was Lieutenant Colonel Gregory Gaskin.

In 1979, Lieutenant Colonel Carl Morgan was appointed, the Chief Administrator for Matarkai Garrison; he took over from Lt Col Gaskin.

In 1981, Lt Col Morgan handed over the administration of Matarkai Garrison to Lt Col Claude St. Romaine.

In 1984, the Government established the Hydro Electric Project at Matarkai Garrison. The name of the Hydro Electric Project was Eclipse Falls Hydro Electric Project (EFHEP.) Colonel Desmond Roberts was given the responsibility for EFHEP. A number of technicians from the Georgetown Power House, the Guyana Technical Institute, and the GDF Engineer Command, were sent to Matarkai to work on the project. In addition, approximately forty North Korean citizens arrived in Guyana to work on the project.

In 1986, as Deputy Commander of the Ground Forces Group (all the Battalions in the GDF), I visited Matarkai Garrison to inspect 4 Company. I met Col. Roberts at Arakaka on the Barima River. At the location, Major Huburn Humphrey, and members of the Engineers Command; were launching a steel bridge across the Barima River. After the launching of the Bridge, I travelled back by land rover to Matthews Ridge with Col. Roberts. During the trip, he told me that President Desmond Hoyte had terminated the Eclipse Hydro project and had ordered Hamilton Green whom he had sent to the area and himself to return to Georgetown.

Further, he had ordered Col. Roberts to retrench half of the workers at Matarkai Garrison, and he complied with his orders.

Subsequently, President Hoyte ordered all the North Korean citizens to leave Guyana.

In January 1987, I was appointed Chief Administrator of Matarkai Garrison, and took over the administration from Lt. Col. Claude St. Romaine. In addition to my responsibilities, as Chief Administrator, I was the Official Government Gazetted Land and Mines Officer; it was for an area for about thirty square miles, from Five Star Village in the West, to Port Kaituma in the East. Over and above, I was the Guyana Gold Board representative for the area. To execute my title role, I was given five hundred thousand dollars, to purchase gold for the Gold Board.

The mandate was for all the gold miners, to sell their gold to the Gold Board. On taking over Matarkai Garrison, I was responsible for a twenty- two mile /35 km railroad that extended from Matthews Ridge to Port Kaituma.

Further, I was responsible, for all the buildings that were owned by Matarkai Garrison, at Matthews Ridge, Arakaka and Port Kaituma. At Matthews Ridge, the local residents lived on two hills in the village. The names of the hills are Heaven Hill and Hell Hill. On Heaven Hill, there is a Community Centre, a Primary School, and a Post Office. Also, approximately thirty buildings that included residences and business places; that the local residents owned. On Hell Hill is the Matthews Ridge Police Station, a number of three bedroom buildings and business places.

On the main road, there is a small Church and a number of business places. At Pakera, is the Matthews Ridge Hospital; with twenty-four patients' beds. There is a residence for the doctor and the nurses. Also at Pakera, there is a pumping station for water and a reservoir. This pumping station, during the days of the manganese company pumped water to the washing plant. Although the four pumps were functional, they were not being utilized. The residents, of Matthews Ridge, received their water supply from two artesian wells.

Up on 'The Ridge' there are three hills. Hill 1 is the highest point on Matarkai Garrison. On Hill 1, are the Guyana House, the Chief Administrators' home and four guest houses. Three of them had three bedrooms, and one had two bedrooms. On Hill 2, there are twelve buildings; four of them had housed the GDF Soldiers, and eight others were the accommodations for senior workers of Matarkai Garrison. On Hill 3 is the administrative building with several offices. They are the finance, auditors, secretarial, and the chief administrator offices. There is also a building for the Magistrate Court. At the time, the visiting Magistrate was Stephen Knights, a former GDF Officer. He normally visited Matarkai Garrison once a month.

In the railroad yard, there was a railroad office, a large ordinance store, a powerhouse with three diesel generators; as well as, a mechanical workshop that catered for the train and vehicles, an electrical workshop, and a carpenter shop. At Papaya, there is a sawmill, and at Matthews Ridge, there is a cassava mill and a small herd of cattle. At Arakaka; Matarkai Garrison owned twelve buildings that were homes for the local residents. At Port Kaituma there is a power plant, a water plant, a multilateral school, a number of buildings that were homes for the teachers, a cassava mill, a guesthouse, and a port.

Subsequent to taking over Matarkai Garrison in January 1987, I attended a GDF Financial Conference. While at the conference, the GDF Commander, Brigadier General David Granger, awarded Matarkai Garrison one million dollars. The money was required to pay, the salaries of one hundred and thirty civilian employees at Matarkai Garrison for one year. Likewise, it was to buy one shipment of diesel fuel, for that same period.

In March 1987, I realized that the big gold miners; had not brought their gold for sale to the Gold Board. They were not acquiescent in past, because the former Chief Administrator, Lt. Col St. Romanie was also a gold miner. Only the small miners were compliant, and had brought their gold to the Gold Board. The gold that they brought to be sold, were in the amounts of pennyweights. At a later time, I learned that three miners had gone to the airport to travel to Georgetown. I went to the airport and met them; I enquired if they had any gold to declare and they responded "no". Subsequently, the soldiers who lived on the Hill, above the airport building informed me that the miners had hidden their gold under the airport building. I told the soldiers to retrieve the gold from under the building, and I took the gold to my office. In my office, I had the equipment to burn, extract the impurities and weigh the gold. Once, this process was completed the gold only weighed fifteen ounces. I paid the monetary value of the gold to the soldiers.

Shortly afterwards, the miners came to my office demanding their gold. I told them they had not declared any gold; therefore, the gold that was hidden under the airport building had been confiscated. After that incident, most of the big gold miners brought some of their gold for sale to the Gold Board. The gold that the miners, brought to the Gold Board was in excess of the five hundred thousand dollars, that the Gold Board had given me to purchase gold. Sometimes, the amount of gold sold was two million dollars or more, so I gave the miners promissory notes for their gold. I took the gold to Georgetown, and sold it to the Gold Board. On my return to Matthews Ridge, I paid the miners for their gold.

In 1988, the GDF did not allocate any money to Matarkai Garrison. Consequently, I had to appeal to the Regional Chairman, Mr. Barrington Warde for financial assistance to pay the civilian employees. As a result, Mr. Barrington Warde and I went to Georgetown, to meet with Mr. Ramchand at the Ministry of Finance Office, in South Road, Georgetown. I gave Mr. Ramchand, a list with all the names and salaries, of the civilian employees at Matarkai Garrison. Thus, he allocated the salaries for the civilian employees on a monthly basis. I gave the responsibility, of collecting the salaries to one of my assistants Mr. Egan Bazillio. Futhermore, there was no money for me to purchase fuel, or conduct any other business for Matarkai Garrison.

At that stage, I decided to sell all the houses at Matarkai Garrison, to the residents who lived in them. I had a meeting with my financial staff; at the meeting, we decided to have the properties appraised to ascertain their value. Once we concluded this process, I sold the one-bedroom houses for fifteen thousand dollars; the two bedroom houses for twenty thousand dollars, and the three bedroom houses for thirty thousand dollars. This decision proved to be successful. As a result, Matarkai Garrison got the finances it needed, and the ability to continue functioning without hindrances; to its daily operations for one year. Moreover, Matarkai Garrison was able to purchase several shipments of diesel fuel for the Garrison. As well as, I paid the contractors to cut the bushes that hung over the railroad; purchase sleepers for the railway and spare parts for the train engine.

Further, in 1988 Brig. Gen. Granger, Force Commander of the GDF, left to attend the University of Guyana to earn his Master of Arts degree in history. Major Gen. McLean, Chief of Staff (COS) was also Chairman of the Guyana Cricket Board. Therefore, every time the COS left the Country to attend a cricket conference or any other GDF business, the Director General of the Guyana National Service, Col. Joseph Singh acted as COS. On those occasions, he became the liaison between the GDF and President Desmond Hoyte. Intrinsically, these interactions enhanced his relationship with President Hoyte and he was viewed more favourably. As it was in 1988, in 1989, the GDF did not allocate any funds for Matarkai Garrison. As a consequence, I decided to sell all the derelict vehicles at

Matarkai Garrison. I sold a local businessman the saw mill, and a small herd of cattle to local residents. With the money from the sales of these assets, it was feasible for me to purchase fuel for 1989 and continue my daily tasks of managing Matarkai Garrison.

In August 1989, I left Guyana for England and the United States of America on vacation leave. When I returned to Guyana, I resumed my duties at Matarkai Garrison. For the duration of my absence, Mr. Egan Bazillio acted as the Chief Administrator, and Mr. Desmond Hall purchased gold for the Gold Board. During that time, the miners sold very little gold to Mr. Hall for the Gold Board. As a result of my presence, the miners again started selling gold to the Gold Board. In November 1989, the COS Major General McLean, attained the age of fifty-five years old. He indicated to President Hoyte that he would be retiring. President Hoyte, then summoned Brig. Gen. Grainger, Force Commander of the GDF to his office. Brig. Gen. Grainger was informed that he was appointing Col. Singh as COS of the GDF.

On January 2nd, 1990, Maj. Gen. McLean retired from the GDF. Thus, Col. Singh was appointed COS of the GDF, with the rank of Brigadier General. Consequently, this meant that Col. Singh had by-passed Brig. Gen. Granger, Col. Morgan, Col. Roberts and Col. Martindale who were his seniors. Brig. General Granger was then appointed National Security advisor to President Hoyte.

I must state, that during my tour of duty at Matarkai Garrison from 1987 and to late 1989, no Senior Officers from the GDF ever visited Matarkai Garrison. The only Government officials, to visit Matarkai Garrison were the Minister of Health Mr. Noel Blackman, and the Minister of Finance Mr. Carl Greenidge. In addition, the Regional Chairman Mr. Barrington Warde was a frequent visitor to Matarkai Garrison.

On January 1st 1990, I attained the age of fifty-five, and was required to retire from the GDF; it was the mandate for all officers. However, no one asked me to resign, and by March 1990, I retired from the GDF. At the time of my retirement, I was the most decorated officer or soldier in the GDF and as of this writing, the only one awarded a medal for Valor

The medals I was awarded are the Independence Medal, Military Service Medal (MSM) for Valour, Jaguar Medal, Border Defence Medal and Military Efficiency Medal.

In actual fact, every officer who has served twenty years in the GDF is normally awarded the Military Service Medal (MSM). I am the first recipient of the MSM for actions in New River on August 19, 1969 while a non-commissioned officer.

The administration did not want to award me the Military Service Star (MSS) is the highest award presented to 'Officers' for exceptional service, above and beyond the call of duty or for gallantry in action. As of this writing, it has only been awarded to those officers who have achieved the title of Chief-of-Staff. For my twenty years of honourable service, instead, I was awarded a GDF gold tie pin.

On my retirement, I was awarded a special medal for my twenty-five years of service.

Chapter 16

Miscarriage of Justice

In 1995, Deputy Chief-of-Staff, Colonel Godwyn McPherson took command of the Guyana Defence Force after Chief-of Staff (COS) Brigadier General Joseph Singh, departed to attend the Royal College of Defence Studies at Belgrave Square, UK. Upon the return of Brig. General Singh, he immediately questioned the financial actions of his Deputy, Colonel McPherson and that of the Quarter Master General and Accountant, Colonel Allan Lewis, by hastily referring his perceived concerns of financial irregularities to the Guyana Police Force (GPF), rather than first requesting the customary and established in-house investigation, as was done with others.

Both Colonel's McPherson and Lewis were sent on Administrative leave, for their actions pertaining to budgetary matters that were previously considered routine and acceptable. The routine and acceptable policy followed when the force has exhausted its annual budget to meet on-going expenses is to borrow from the GDF Funds to satisfy those expenses.

It should be noted, the 'seed money' for the GDF Funds primarily originated from contributions made by its members, and all funds borrowed for the force expenses were always reimbursed in full from the subsequent year's Parliamentary approved budget.

The actions taken against Colonels McPherson and Lewis without the customary and in-house investigations created much consternation/dismay among the officers and ranks, prompting most to describe the actions of the COS as political opportunism.

The Police investigation took approximately two (2) years to complete and sometime during that period, both Colonels McPherson and Lewis were suspended without pay.

Colonels McPherson and Lewis were replaced in the Force by Lieutenant Colonels Michael Atherly and Lennox Wilson respectively, and both subsequently were promoted to Colonels.

At the end of the Police investigation, Colonel Godwyn McPherson and Colonel Allan Lewis were vindicated and reinstated in the Defence Force but never returned to the positions they previously held.

Colonels McPherson and Lewis are now deceased.

Chapter 17

Tribute to a Soldier

His Excellency President David A. Granger Retired Brigadier General

President David Arthur Granger takes Presidential Salute at Consecration and Trooping of the Colours Ceremony with Chief of Staff, Brig. General Mark Phillips on August 18, 2015.

"Trooping the Colours" is a ceremony involving parading the Colours which identifies the Units, developed initially as a means of ensuring that each soldier knew the colour of his unit and could therefore rally in battle. However, Colours are no longer carried into battle in response to the changing circumstances of war.

His Excellency, President David Arthur Granger won the May 11, 2015 General Elections in Guyana and on May 16, was sworn in on the balcony of the Parliament as Guyana's 8th Executive President, Commander-in- Chief of the Armed Forces and Head of State of the Cooperative Republic of Guyana. It has been several years since such a momentous occasion was held at Public Buildings as it is traditionally observed at State House.

His official inauguration was celebrated on Independence Day, May 26 at National Stadium.

In 1994, Brigade General Granger retired from military service after serving as National Security Adviser to the President (1990-94) and as Commander of the GDF (1979-90).

The retired Brigadier General campaigned on a platform of increased security, fighting drugs and human trafficking.

His cabinet includes former Chief-of-Staffs and other Army officers:

Lt. Col. (Ret) Joseph Harmon, Minister of the Presidency.

Lt. (Ret) Mark Archer – Director of Communications at the President's Office.

Brig. Gen. (Ret) Edward Collins, National Security Advisor.

Maj. Gen. (Ret) Joseph G. Singh, Chairman of Task Force Commission – Project Restore Guyana.

Maj. Gen. (Ret) Michael Atherly, Head of National Anti-Narcotics Agency.

Rear Adm. (Ret) Gary Best – Presidential Advisor on the Environment.

W/Lt. (Ret) Clarissa S. Hookumchand-Riehl - Ambassador to Canada.

Chapter 18

A Soldier of Valour

A professional soldier's life does not fit easily into a biography unless the soldier is a senior commander, and then the biography centers on grand strategy and not the coarse details of the battlefield and/or the combat infantryman in the field.

The author and soldier, Compton Hartley Liverpool as of this writing is one of the Army's (Guyana Defence Force) most decorated officer/soldier and the proud recipient of the Military Service Medal (MSM) for Valour for his actions on the early morning of Tuesday, August 19, 1969 – his heroics in New River (Operation Climax) is a powerful credential !

Lt. Col. Compton Hartley Liverpool (Ret) was born on January 1, 1936 in Lacytown, Georgetown, Guyana (formerly British Guiana).

In 1955, he started his military career when he joined the then British Guiana Volunteer Force (BGVF) and was assigned to Company C as a Private.

During his Military career he rose from a Private to a Lieutenant Colonel on soldierly abilities alone, learning each day. He also successfully completed several military courses and achieved many first (1st) during his career.

On the birth of the Guyana Defence Force (GDF) on November 1, 1965, he transitioned into the newly established Force as a Corporal; attended the Conversion Course where he was adjudged the best student and promoted to Sergeant. Immediately thereafter, he became the 1st Platoon Sergeant of the 1st Recruit Platoon trained by personnel from the British Army.

1966 – He was assigned to B (2nd) Company as a Platoon Sergeant.

Oct 1966 – He was sent on the 1st Senior Non Commissioned Officers (NCO) course held at Atkinson Field now Camp Stephenson, and Tacama Battle School, Berbice River. At the end of that training, he was adjudged the best student and assigned to the Training Wing, Atkinson Field as an instructor.

May   1967   He was promoted from Sergeant to Warrant Officer II

October	1967	while holding the Rank of WO II, he was transferred from the Training Wing and assigned to B (2nd) Company, as Commander of the 3rd Platoon.
December	1967	He was appointed the 1st Guyanese Company Sergeant Major (CSM).
May/October	1968	He was sent to the UK to complete the following three (3) courses:

1) All Arms Drill Course at The Grenadier Guards Barracks in Caterham, Surrey. He was the first Guyanese to win the 'Best Student Cup'.

2) Senior NCO Weapons & Tactics Course in Brecon, South Wales.

3) Parachute Course with the Royal Air Force (RAF) in Abingdon, Oxfordshire where he earned his Parachute Wing.

October 1968 – Upon his return to Guyana, he was assigned to A Company as the Company Sergeant Major (CSM).

In addition, he was a founding member of the Army's newly established Rugby that subsequently went undefeated for many years.

August 19, 1969 – During the New River Operation (Operation Climax), he distinguished himself by gallant, intrepid (resolutely fearless) actions while performing the duties of a nose gunner aboard a reconfigured civilian passenger DHC – 6 De Havilland (Twin Otter) aircraft during a 90 mile flight from Apoteri, Rupununi River armed with a General Purpose Machine Gun (GPMG) and a Self- Loading Rifle (SLR) to the area of operation (AO).

His bold action and heroic disregard for his own safety while in flight and providing "AERIAL FIRE" was directly responsible for the Army's success in removing the armed and occupying Surinamese soldiers and Djukas from the Nation's sovereign territory.

May 1970	He was awarded the Military Service Medal (MSM) for VALOUR by President Arthur R. Chung
Dec 1970	The Scarlet Beret (a GDF Newspaper) named him – "Soldier of the Year."
Jan 1971	He was Commissioned as a Lieutenant (subaltern) and assigned as a Platoon Commander in B Company
1972	Appointed Officer Commanding Recruiting Division of the Training Wing.
1973	Appointed C Company Commander and authorized to wear the rank of Captain. As Commanding Officer, he led his Company to the 1st Drill competition victory.
Jan 1974	Appointed Commander of B Company
July 1974	Seconded to National Services as Training Officer and Officer Commanding the Pioneer Corps.
March 1975	Promoted to Major and appointed Center Administrator of Papaya Training Center, Matthews Ridge area with a staff of 200, and 1,000 + pioneers.

September 1976	He returned to the GDF and appointed Base Commander of Camp Ayanganna with Rank of Captain. He was also 2nd in Command of the Logistics Command.
January 1978 -	Promoted to Major and assigned to the Training Wing.
October 1978 -	Participated in a 5 week troop exchange program with The Black Watch (Royal Highland) Regiment, UK where he led a 120 man Labaria Company of the GDF to Catterick, Surrey. He remained in the UK for an additional 5 weeks to complete the Combat Team Commanders course in Warminster.
February 1979	After returning from the UK, he was appointed Base Commander at Camp Stephenson.
July 1979	Appointed Commanding Officer of Perai (12th Infantry) Battalion. Under his command, the Battalion won the competition In August 1980 and was elected the best in the Force.
1981 -	He returned to the Training Corp as Commanding Officer (CO) while handing over command of the Perai Battalion.
July 1981/May 1982	He was sent to Canada to attend Canadian Land Forces Staff School in Toronto, and the Canadian Command & Staff College in Kingston, ON

May 1982	Upon his return from Canada, he was appointed 1st Commander of the newly Established Special Forces Battalion that included Land, Sea and Air Units – Reconnaissance Squadron, Air, Jungle Company, Land; Marine Raiders, Sea.
1983	Appointed Commander of the 13th Guard Battalion (An all Government Ceremonial Unit), and promoted to Lt. Colonel. The Unit won the second Drill competition.
1984	Selected by President L. F. S. Burnham as his Aide-de-Camp (ADC) for Official State visits to Bulgaria, Ukraine and China.
1985	Mr. Desmond Hoyt succeeded Mr. Burnham as President of the Nation after the passing of Mr. Burnham and the 13th Guard Battalion was disbanded. He was then appointed 2nd in Command of Ground Forces Group (all Battalions under one Commander).
1987	Appointed Chief Administrator of MATARKI (Matthews Ridge/ Arakaka / Kaituma) Garrison.
1990	He retired under the mandatory retirement age of 55 after 25 years of active service in the Defence Force.

Decorations, Medals, Badges:

Independence Medal -1966

Parachute Badge -1968

Jaguar Medal - 1970

Military Service Medal (MSM) 1970

Border Defence Medal

Military Efficiency Medal 1990

Chapter 19

50th Anniversary of the Guyana Defence Force

The 50th Anniversary Church Service

The celebration of the 50th anniversary of the Guyana Defence Force (GDF) commenced on Sunday, November 1st, 2015, with a church service at the National Cultural Centre, located on Homestretch Avenue, Georgetown. The ceremony was attended by the Chief of Staff (COS) Brigadier General Mark Phillips, former Chief of Staffs Major General Norman McLean, Major General Michael Atherly, Brigadier General Edward Collins and Rear Admiral Gary Best, and Brigadier General (Ret) Jullian Bruce Lovell. Also, present were retired Colonels Cecil Martindale, Windee Algernon, Frank Bisphan, Lawrence Paul, and Enoch Gaskin. As well as Retired Lieutenant Colonels Compton Hartley Liverpool, Fairbairn Liverpool, Hyacinth King, Victor Wilson, Fitzroy Griffith, Minister of State Minister of State Joseph Harmon, and other Senior Officers, Junior Officers, Others Ranks, Veterans of the GDF, Canadian Delegation of the Guyana Ex-Soldiers Association of Canada, Captain John DaSilva, Lieutenant Michael Narain, and Corporals Ingrid Ifill and Pertab Singh. Also present were Heads of the Discipline

Services, the Commissioner of Police Seelall Persaud, Director of Prisons Dale Erskine, and Fire Chief Mr. Marlon Gentle, Ministers of the Government, Members of the Government, Members of the Diplomatic Corps, and invited guests.

The service began with the Nation Anthem being played by the Guyana Defence Force Band, on the arrival of His Excellency, The President of Guyana Brigadier General (Ret) David Granger and Commander-in-Chief (CIC) of the Armed Forces. After the National Anthem, the Regimental Colours was paraded into the National Cultural Centre and placed on the stage. A Muslim cleric, a Hindu Cleric and a Christian Minister said the prayers. The scriptures were read by three GDF soldiers. The audience sung two national songs, My Native Land, My Guyana Eldorado, and the hymn, Amazing Grace. The main sermon was delivered by Warrant Officer (Ret) Ronald Reyonlds, the Deacon of St. Sidwell's Anglican Church. After the sermon, the Chief of Staff in his address gave an outline on the history of the GDF. His Excellency President Granger was the final speaker, and in his address he congratulated the GDF, on its fifty years of commitment to the defence of Guyana. Further, he stated that November 1st of each year will be observed as Veterans Day in Guyana. After his address, the ceremony was concluded with the singing of the National Anthem.

Remembrance Day Service

On Sunday November 8th, 2015 the Remembrance Day Service was held at the Cenotaphs of WW1 and WW 11 soldiers, at the junction of Church and Main Streets Georgetown. In attendance were the Chief of Staff (COS) Brigadier General Mark Phillips, President of the Veterans Legion of Guyana, Lieutenant (Ret) George Gomes, His Worship the Mayor of Georgetown, Hamilton Green, Heads of the Discipline Services, The Commissioner of Police Seelall Persaud, Director of Prisons Dale Erskine, Fire Chief Mr. Marlon Gentle, Ministers of the Government, Members of the Government, Members of the Diplomatic Corps, former Chief of Staffs, and other Senior Officers of the GDF, and a wide cross section of the Guyanese populace. The service began with the Nation Anthem, being played by Guyana Police Force Band on the arrival His Excellency, The President of Guyana Brigadier General (Ret) David Granger and Commander-in-Chief of the Armed Forces. After the National Anthem, the last post was sounded by a bugler (a tribute to the war dead), followed by the reveille, and then a minute of silence was observed. A Muslim Cleric, a Hindu Cleric, and a Christian Minister said the prayers; then there was the laying of the wreaths at the Cenotaphs.

The first wreath was laid by His Excellency President David Granger, and followed by the Chief of Staff, the President of Guyana Veterans Legion, His Worship the Mayor of Georgetown, Heads of the Discipline Services, and Members of the Diplomatic Corp. The hymn, Abide With Me was sung by the audience. His Excellency President Granger in his address, paid tribute to the soldiers of WW1 and WW 11, who made the ultimate sacrifice for freedom in the world. At the conclusion, of the service the National Anthem was sung; then there was a parade by the Joint Services. The parade was led by the members of the Veterans Legion that included twenty ex-soldiers of WW11. They were all in wheelchairs to participate in the parade. The parade marched down Main Street, and His Excellency President Granger took the salute at the gate of State House.

The Reception at Coghlan House

A reception was held at Coghlan House, Headquarters of the Guyana Veterans Legion after the parade, for all the dignitaries and other invited guests. In attendance were the COS Brigadier General Mark Phillips, President of the Veterans Legion of Guyana, Lieutenant (Ret) George Gomes, former Chief of Staffs Major General Michael Atherly, Brigadier General Edward Collins and Rear Admiral Gary Best, and also Brigadier General

(Ret) Jullian Bruce Lovell. As well as, and retired Colonels Cecil Martindale, Frank Bisphan and Lawrence Paul. Also present were retired Lieutenant Colonels Compton Hartley Liverpool, Fairbairn E. Liverpool, Hyacinth King, Victor Wilson, Fitzroy Griffith, and Minister of State Lieutenant Colonel (Ret) Joseph Harmon. Also, there were Other Senior Officers and Veterans of the GDF, Canadian Delegation of the Guyana Ex-Soldiers Association of Canada. As well as, The Director of Prisons, Mr. Dale Erskine and Fire Chief Mr. Marlon Gentle. The British High Commissioner, Mr. Greg Quinn, and invited guests. Also present, were twenty Ex-servicemen from WW 11. The reception commenced, with the singing of the National Anthem by the audience, accompanied by Guyana Police Force Steel Band, on the arrival of His Excellency President David Granger, Commander -in-Chief, Brigadier General (Ret.) The last post was sounded by a GDF bugler; followed the reveille, and a minute of silence was observed. Prayers were offered by a Muslim Cleric, a Hindu Cleric, and a Christian Minister.

Subsequently, three Guyana National songs were sung, they were My Native Land, My Guyana Eldorado and O Beautiful Guyana. These songs were accompanied by the Guyana Police Force (GPF) Steel Band. Afterwards, the President of the Guyana Veterans Legion; gave an overview of his three years as its President, and the services that are being rendered to the veterans who are never able to leave their home; especially because of illness or lack of physical mobility. He also requested that a Veterans Commission, be established and based at Coghlan House. His Excellency President David Granger, in his address applauded the Veterans Legion for its hard work throughout the years. He also mentioned that a Veterans Commission will be established, and the office will be stationed at Base Camp Ayanganna, Thomas Lands, Georgetown.

His Excellency President David Granger presented the Guyana Veterans Legion, with a cheque for four million dollars, The

Chief of Staff, 1 million dollars; the Director of Prisons, one hundred thousand dollars, Minister of State, Joseph Harmon, one hundred thousand dollars, the Fire Chief, fifty thousand dollars, and many contributions from retired Senior Officers of the GDF. The reception concluded, with the audience singing Guyana's National Anthem.

The Beauty Pageant

On Wednesday, November 11, 2015, the Miss Guyana Defence Force 2015 Beauty Pageant finals, was held at the National Cultural Centre. Prior, to the final night of the competitions; there were nineteen contestants of the Women Army Corps (WAC) who participated, for the coveted crown, of Miss Guyana Defence Force 2015. Commanding Officer of the Women Army Corps (WAC) Lieutenant Colonel Natasha Stanford respectfully indicated; that events of the pageant, were unconventional in comparison, to other mainstream beauty contests. The pageant contestants were required to exhibit their personal talents, sensitivity, eloquence, and intelligence; as well as, demonstrate their military skills. The events entailed a Run and Shoot Competition; to determine their physical fitness and marksmanship aptitudes.

The highlight of the festivities; were the contestants who appeared on stage with elegance and glamour; as each of them gave a personal introduction to the audience. The evening was permeated with excitement, as the contestants paraded in the swimsuits; there were various individual performances, and an exciting exhibition by a bodybuilder, and current Mr. GDF, Sergeant Davis of 31 Special Forces Squadron. In addition, a dance sequence by members of the National School of Dance, enticed the audience, who were waiting excitedly on the Evening Gown and Intelligence events of the pageant. The contestants were resplendent in their evening gowns. The next phase was the intelligence questions, to determine the winner of the contest. Afterwards, the judges decided on the final five contestants.

They runners-up were categorically selected: Miss Training Corps, Lance Corporal (L/Cpl) Letitia Miles was the first runner-up and won the Best Fitness Title, Ms. Base Camp Stephenson, Pte. Fomba Ramsay was the second runner-up and won the Best Talent Title, Ms. Air Corp, (L/CPL) Tiffany Smith was the third runner up and won the Best Body Title, Ms. G6 Branch, (L/CPL) Alicia Jack, was the fourth runner-up and won Ms. Congeniality Title, and Ms. Base Camp Ayanganna, (L/CPL) Carlesia Laundry won the Best Smile Title.

Lance Corporal (L/ Cpl) Daniella Castillon, Miss Sports Department, won the coveted title of Miss. Guyana Defence Force (GDF) 2015. She was crowned by the former Ms. GDF (2012), Sergeant Shamekia Devonish and given the keys to a new automobile. In conclusion, it was a glamourous and memorable night.

The Parade

On November 14th, 2015 the Guyana Defence Force (GDF) held an early morning parade through the streets of the Capital City Georgetown. The GDF troops assembled at Camp Ayanganna, then accompanied by the military band of the GDF, marched west along Thomas Road to Camp St, turning south to follow Camp St. to Durban St. At Durban St., the parade went east to Vlissingen Road where it turned north towards the Square of the Revolution that is situated at Vlissingen Rd. and Brickdam. At the Square of the Revolution, His Excellency President General David Granger and Commander- in-Chief, Retired Brigadier General of the GDF took the salute from the detachments marching past.

That same afternoon, a delegation of 50 members of the XGDF Association of New York led by its President Ms. Cheryl Tappin, flew in to Guyana to participate in the GDF's 50th Anniversary activities. The delegation's first official duty occurred on the 16th when it was welcomed by the GDF Chief of Staff Brigadier General Mark Phillips at his office in Camp Ayanganna. As part of the lively interaction between the Chief of Staff and the visitors, most of whom would have been known to him from their time in the army. A commemoration gifts and tokens of honour were exchanged; then photographs were taken with Brigadier General Phillips and his Staff.

Some members of the delegation paid a courtesy call on His Excellency the President of Guyana David A. Granger on the 18th of November at his Vlissingen Road office. The leader of XGDF of New York's delegation Cheryl Tappin, took this opportunity to present His Excellency President David Granger, with a jacket bearing the crest of the Association, as well as his portrait painted by New York based ex-soldier Oswald Mussenden. During this meeting with His Excellency President David Granger's grave concerns were expressed about the issues of poverty and poor education in Guyana. The delegation resolved at His Excellency David Granger's urging, to assist in bringing about positive change in these areas.

Trooping of the Colours

The Origins of Colours - From the earlier times, men have carried into battle some token to serve as a rallying point and for identification in the field. The form this has taken has varied through the world. When, however, troop were hurriedly raised in England to meet the threat of the Spanish Armada, the local leaders, being of yeoman stock (an attendant or officer in a noble household) therefore bearing no coat of arms, they used flags, each of a different colour, to distinguish their commands. Thus this token took the shape of a flag, and became known as a "Colour".

During the afternoon on November 18th 2015, the Guyana Defence Force held the long established military ceremony known as the Trooping of the Colours, where the Regiment assembles in formal order to view and remember its battle flags (The Colours) which are paraded through the ranks so that each soldier can observe them in its entirety. Among the dignitaries in attendance as guests of the Chief of Staff Brigadier General Mark Phillips, were retired Generals and former Chiefs of Staff Norman McLean, Joseph Singh, Micheal Atherly, Edward Collins and retired Rear Admiral Gary Best. Many former senior officers of the GDF such as Brigadier General Jullian Bruce Lovell, Colonels Cecil Martindale, Frank Bispham, Lawrence Paul, Enoch Gaskin, Windee Algernon, Compton Hartley Liverpool, Fairbairn Liverpool, Victor Wilson, Fitzroy Griffith, Hyacinth King and Joseph Harmon the current Minister of State, were in attendance; along with large numbers of serving or former ranks of the GDF, overseas delegations, as well as members of the Government and the citizenry.

The parade, commanded by Major Kennard Liverpool, and consisting of five detachments representing Camp Ayanganna, Camp Stephenson, 1st Battalion GDF, 2nd Battalion GDF, and 4th Engineers Battalion, marched on to the square at Camp Ayanganna and took up their positions. The Unit Colours for the five detachments on parade were then consecrated by a Muslim cleric, a Hindu cleric, and a Christian Minister, before being borne by five subalterns to positions in front of their respective units.

After the inspection, His Excellency President David A. Granger gave permission for the parade to continue. Each detachment then marched past His Excellency President David Granger in line abreast, unit flags out front and center, first in slow time, then again in quick time, each time executing the "Eyes right" salute as they went past His Excellency the President. After returning to their original positions, the units faced

His Excellency the President, advanced 15 paces and again saluted by presenting arms. His Excellency President Granger then addressed them, offering congratulations on the excellent display of precision marching; as well as the achievement of the GDF's 50th year in existence. After the speech, the parade was given permission by His Excellency the President to march off the square, which was followed by the band and drums of the GDF led by Lt. Col. Lawrence Bourne "beating the retreat" the final event of the ceremony.

The Culmination

On November 19th 2015, the Guyana Veterans Legion hosted a ceremony in Camp Ayanganna at the Western Gate, where there is a veterans' monument; in remembrance of comrades from the GDF. Those in attendance included the Chief of Staff of the GDF Brigadier General Mark Phillips, President of the Veterans Legion, Retired Lt. Col. George Gomes, Former Chief-of Staffs of the Guyana Defence Force, Retired Lt. Col. Compton Hartley Liverpool, President of the XGDF Association of New York Cheryl Tappin and members of the delegation, Guyana Ex-Soldiers Association of Canada delegate Ingrid Ifill, retired senior officers, retired female pilot Lt. Cheryl Pickering-Moore and veterans of the GDF.

The National Anthem was played on arrival of His Excellency the President of Guyana David Granger, followed by the "last post" and the "reveille" sounded by a bugler, one minute of silence and then prayers by a Muslim cleric, a Hindu cleric, and a Christian Minister. Next there was the wreath laying ceremony at the veterans' monument. His Excellency the President David Granger laid the first wreath; then the Chief of Staff Brigadier Gen. Mark Phillips, President of the Veterans Legion, Retired Lt. Col. George Gomes, retired Lt. Col. Compton Hartley Liverpool, and the President of the XGDF Association of New York Cheryl Tappin.

The gathering was then addressed by retired Lt. Col. Compton Hartley Liverpool who gave an outline of the formative years of the GDF, mentioning that his regimental number was 1010. Likewise, there were speeches given by the President of the XGDF Association of New York Cheryl Tappin, President of the Veterans Legion, Retired Lt. Col. George Gomes and the keynote speaker was Chief of Staff Brigadier Gen. Mark Phillips. After his speech, he presented the Veterans Legion with a donation of one million dollars. Further presentations of commemorative caps, were presented to the nine original soldiers of the GDF including retired Lt. Col. Compton Hartley Liverpool. His Excellency President David Granger did not speak at this ceremony, but he congratulated the nine soldiers for fifty years of service to the GDF.

The next day, on November 20th, 2015 the GDF held a Military Tattoo on the Camp Ayanganna playing field, where it could display the skills of its members for the edification and entertainment of the public. The attendees at this sporting event included former senior officers, soldiers, dignitaries and guests as in the two previous ceremonies for the 50th anniversary observances.

The event commenced with a spectacular parachute jump conducted by the 31 Special Force Squadron, where 15 of its members free-fell from 7000ft, opening their parachutes at 2000ft before gliding into landings in front of the audience. Then the Women's Army Corp and recruits conducted silent drills (without words commands) and precision weapons drills; followed by a mock battle by 31 Special Force Squadron, followed by the Drums and Band "Beat the Retreat". The Military Tattoo ended with a display of fireworks conducted by the Artillery Squadron.

The final official event of the GDF 50th Anniversary celebrations on 26th November was a quarterly fitness competition held at Camp Stephenson, Timehri. Essentially, all units of the GDF were participants in the competition. The event, known to soldiers as a "run and shoot", required that teams of 6 representing each unit first run a distance of approximately 5 miles to the rifle ranges then fire live rounds at various targets between 100 yards and 600 yards. 1st and 2nd place winners were units from the 31 Special Force Squadron; third place being occupied by the Training Corps. The Chief-of-Staff Brigadier General Mark Phillips invited retired Warrant Officer 1 Joseph Glasgow, former Regimental Sergeant Major (RSM), of 3 Special Forces Battalion, a member of the XGDF NY delegation, to present a trophy to the winning team. This was the conclusion of the GDF 50th Anniversary celebrations.

PART TWO

Chapter 20

G2 Intelligence and Security

The Guyana Defence Force 'Intelligence Section' commenced its basis intelligence course training in 1966, when the British Garrison was withdrawing from British Guiana. The course was conducted by British Army Captain Peter Cullen, GSO 3 Intelligence, at the then Garrison HQ on Young Street, Eve Leary, where the Criminal Investigation Department (CID) of the Guyana Police Force is now located.

It should be noted, before the Nation's Independence on May 26, 1966, all Intelligence was handled by the Special Branch of the Police Force (Special Branch is a label customarily used to identify units responsible for matters of national security in British and Commonwealth Police Forces), and most of their operations were limited to the Coastal region and McKenzie/

Wismar and Christianburg. These areas are now known as Linden with little operations in the hinterland locations.

When the British Army was deployed to British Guiana during the disturbance of February 1962, Garrison Headquarters was established. Also, the Garrison established its own intelligence section working closely with the Special Branch which at that time was headed by a British Police Officer, Robert (Robbie) C. Thom.

The 1966 GDF team was headed by Lt. Carl Morgan and included members of the Ranks, Cecil Austin, Douglas Fletchman, Austin Hughes, Embrach, Vaughn, and others.

The Intelligence Section was later moved from Eve Leary to the lower flat, West wing of the Administration Building of Thomas Lands now Camp Ayanganna.

In 1967, Lt. Morgan handed over the 'Intelligence Section' to Lt. Keith Dyer.

Lt. Dyer was subsequently succeeded by Lt. Oliver Hinckson.

In 1977, General Staff Officer Grade 1 (GSO 1) [Co-ordinator]) Morgan produced the GDF Manual of Staff Duties.

During the early 1980's the name changed to Intelligence Command, which was also commanded by a Commanding Officer.

After a second review in 1990, the name changed to its current name, the G2 Branch, which was and is currently commanded by a Staff Officer 1 General 2.

ROLE OF THE G2 BRANCH

Since the establishment of the GDF the role of the G2 Branch remained constant that is: To provide intelligence and security advice to the Chief of Staff and Units of the Force.

ORGANISATION

The intelligence organization was divided into four main divisions:

Military Police Corps.
Analysis and Production.
Training and Education.
Unit Operations.

It provided staff for operations rooms at Unit and Force levels and all other trained intelligence personnel throughout the Force down to Company level.

THE MILITARY POLICE CORPS

Role: To maintain discipline by the prevention and detection of crime and apprehension of offenders.

To assist in administration and security duties by undertaking fire prevention, traffic control and compound guard duties.

Organisation: This Corps had a 'Dog Wing' for compound guard and security dogs to assist in security work. This Corps had elements in the main GDF bases and interior locations. As the security division of the Intelligence Corps it was directly controlled by the Force Intelligent Officer and managed a small detention centre for military offenders

COMMANDERS

The following Officers served as Commanding Officers of the Intelligence Corps/G2 Branch in the order.

Ret. Colonel Godwin McPherson.
Ret. Brigadier David Granger -1978 - 1979.
Ret. Colonel G. McPherson.
Ret. Lieutenant Colonel Joseph F. Harmon.
Ret. Captain Osborne.
Ex. Captain L. Carroll
Brigadier Edward O. Collins
Ret. Lieutenant Commander A. Edwards.
Colonel Mark Phillips.
W/Lieutenant Colonel Windee Algernon.
Lieutenant Colonel J. Williams.
Lieutenant Colonel G. Lewis.
Lieutenant Colonel S. C. James.

TRAINING

During the early years the Unit was mandated to conduct all operations room courses and security and intelligence courses. These were done at the grades 111 and 11 levels. This training was incorporated with practical exercises on the playfield of

Base Camp Ayanganna in tents. The names of those exercises were "Ex Agoute" and "Ex Running Dog". As part of the training, operatives were exercised in the gathering of intelligence through surveillances and the monitoring of activities. The compilation of village reports was also part of the training then.

DEPLOYMENT

During the deployment of any military contingent a representative from the Intelligence Corps usually accompanied the troops. In those days the representatives were referred to as the "Acorn Rep" or the "India 3Rep". These were signal address group and the call signs used then. "Acorn Reps" and India 3 Reps were deployed on all border locations; they accompanied the GDF front line string band to Nicaragua and Cuba on tour in 1987.

ADMINISTRATIVE CHANGES

During the early days of its establishment the intelligence Corps was seen as the elite arm of the GDF, and special emphasis was paid to the selections of ranks to this Unit. Undesired persons were never transferred from this Unit, but they were struck off strength (SOS). Officers were never rotated. When Officers and Ranks were posted to this Unit, they served until they retired or resigned from the organization.

HOUSING

The Intelligence Corps HQ was located in the administrative building western end on the ground floor. During the 1980's two buildings were allotted to the Corps in Eteringbang Street, Base Camp Ayanganna.

BASE CAMP AYANGANNA

Combat Intelligence, Internal Security Intelligence, Strategic Intelligence and Personnel Section were housed in the allotted buildings while the Headquarters remained in the administrative building.

The Signals Corps

The Signals Corps was established on January 2, 1966. Its initial and introductory course was conducted by a British Army non-commissioned officer, Sergeant Ronald Cameron, Signals Sergeant. The Classes were held in the lecture hall at Thomas Lands now Camp Ayanganna. The GDF members selected to attend the course were Privates Hector Stoute, Douglas Fletchman, Winston Martindale, Monty Lane, Arthur King, Sam Forde, Peter Denny and 2nd Lieutenant Vibart Boodhoo. The course concluded after five weeks of training. The Signallers were dispatched to four locations. Base Camp Ayanganna at Thomas Lands, Base Atkinson Field, East Bank of the Demerara River, and approximately 30 miles South of Camp Ayanganna, the Senior Staff Quarters at Rose Hall Estate on the Corentyne, and Tacama Battle School, 90 miles up the Berbice River.

The radio in use was the SB 22, which was located at Headquarters, Camp Ayanganna. The radio that was used in the field by Rifle Companies was the HF156 radio.

The HF156 radio is an 11 valve High Frequency (HF) transceiver with AM radio telephony and Beat Frequency Oscillator (BFO) with Morse code capabilities.

In October 1966 when the Venezuelans occupy Guyana's half of the Ankoko Island. The GDF established locations at Eteringbang, Kaikan, Kurutoka Villages on the Cuyuni River; Paruima and Kamarang Village on the Kamarang River. A radio net was set up between these five locations.

Also, in November 1967, the GDF established locations at Camp Oronoque and Camp King Fisher in the New River Triangle with communications between these two locations and battalion Headquarters at Timehri.

In January 1969, after the uprising in the Rupununi, the GDF established posts at Lethem, Good Hope, Annai and Orinduik.

Radio network was set up between these locations with Lethem being the Base Station for those locations.

In August 1969 when GDF captured Camp Jaguar; a radio network was established between the Camp and Battalion Headquarters at Timerhi.

In 1970, the GDF occupied locations at Mabaruma and Matthews Ridge. Hence, a radio communication network was set up between those two locations. The GDF now had an established network system between North, East, South and West of Guyana.

In 1972, a Base Station was set up at Training Corps which was linked to Tacama Battle School. In addition, a radio network was established at McKenzie where 7 Company was stationed. By 1978, three locations were established on the Soesdyke, Linden Highway. They were 11 Infantry Battalion at Low Creek, 12 Infantry Battalion at Long Creek and the Archery Battalion at Soweyo. A radio network was set up between these locations. The Signal Corps operated efficiently throughout the entire Guyana and is very active at the present time.

Currently, the radio in use is the Motorola, which replaced the HF156. The Signal Officers of the GDF were Lieutenant Vibart Boodhoo, Lieutenant Randolph Johnson, Lieutenant Compton Ross and Lieutenant Colin Westmoreland.

In 1974, the GDF posted Signallers to the Guyana National Service (GNS). The Guyana National Service (GNS), had links to Base Kimbia; Base Papaya, Tumatumari and Kamarook.

Training Wing – A chronological Summary

TRAINING WING

In January 1966, the Guyana Defence Force (GDF) Training Wing was established at Atkinson Field (now Camp Stephenson) under the leadership of British Army Company Sergeant Major

Instructor (CSM) William Gallagher and Sergeant William Oliver of the 3rd British Parachute Regiment, plus the best Non Commissioned Officers (NCOs) from the British Guyana Volunteer Force (BGVF) that included Eric Primo, Claude McKenzie, Ivan Nichols, Compton Hartley Liverpool, Henry Blackett, Mortimer Niles, Pelham VanCooten, Ulric Sutton, and Cecil Hicks.

During that period, training was also conducted at Thomas Lands (now Camp Ayanganna), Georgetown, and the Battle School at Tacama in the Berbice Savannahs. It should be noted, unlike the 1st Rifle Company was mainly comprised of members of the BGVF, Special Service Unit (SSU) and the British Guyana Police Force (BGPF). The remaining personnel selected for A Company and all subsequent Rifle Companies were drawn from civilian volunteers.

In June 1966, after commanding A Company (Rifle Company), Major Neil Pullen, a British citizen of the Royal East Anglian Regiment, and Aviator, was named Officer Commanding Training Wing. During his command of the Training Wing, A Company, B Company, and C Company Rifle Companies of the 1st Battalion, had completed their training and on October 12, 1966. Those units were placed on high alert and subsequently deployed and/or rotated to the Venezuela Border (Eteringbang) on the Cuyuni River, after Venezuela armed forces seized half of Guyana's Ankoko Island.

A Company was led by British Major Neil Pullen and CSM George Dawes with two Guyanese Platoon Commanders 2nd Lt. Desmond Roberts, 2nd Lt. Ramesh Narine, and two Platoon Sergeants Sergeant Eric Primo and Sgt Claude McKenzie. In June 1966 when Major Neil Pullen left A Company to command the Training Wing, he was replaced by Major Michael Hartland.

B Company was led by British Major Peter Hiscock and CSM Peter Saville with two Guyanese Platoon Commanders and two Platoon Sergeants, 2nd Lt. Asad Ishoof, 2nd Lt. Oscar Pollard, Sergeant Compton Hartley Liverpool and Sgt. Richard Cummings.

C Company was led by British Major Anthony Midford Slade and Company Sergeant Major (CSM) Sandy Duffus, with two Guyanese Platoon Commanders 2nd Lt. Joseph Singh and 2nd Lt. David Granger, and two Platoon Sergeants Sgt Cecil Hicks and Sgt. Henry Blackett.

In October 1966, the first Platoon Sergeant's course was conducted by WO1 William Gallagher and Sgt. William Oliver who were former members of the British Army. The course attendees included 2nd Lt. Keith Dyer, Sgt. Compton Hartley Liverpool, Cpl. Mohamed Kahleel, and Sgt. George Angoy. At the conclusion of the course Sgt. Compton Hartley Liverpool was adjudged the best student and Corporal Mohamed Kahleel was the runner up.

In January 1967, 70 male civilian volunteers were trained to strengthen A, B, and C Rifle Companies that were originally formed with two platoons each.

In February 6, 1967 the Women's Army Corps (WAC's) was establishment and training commenced for its 4 Officers and 60 Other Ranks.

On Monday, March 6, 1967 because of the posting of the best NCO's and men of the BGVF into A Company in November 1965, 50 civilian recruits entered the GDF and were trained as a 'reserve force'; to replace the disbanded Volunteer Force that included 'over age' men. This batch of recruits upon their graduation/passing out parade on Friday, April 7, 1967; merged with eligible members from the BGVF. These recruits were posted to Headquarters (HQ), of 'A', 'C' and 'D' Company located at Eve Leary, Kingston, Georgetown; 'B' company, was posted to New Amsterdam, Berbice, and 'E' company was posted to Mackenzie upper Demerara River.

This batch of 50 recruits, plus the eligible and former members of the BGVF, comprised of 4 Company and 5 Company in the newly formed 2 GDF (2nd Battalion). Further, the unit was recognized as a 'Regular Battalion' rather than a 'Reserve Battalion' as a result of territorial crises during the late 1960's.

The training instructors for this batch included Warrant Officer Eric Primo, Sgt. Willliam Oliver of the 3rd British Parachute Regiment, Sgt. Compton Hartley Liverpool. In 1967, the 1st Champion Non-Commission Officers (NCO) competition took place. Corporal Wilfred Austin of the Reconnaissance Platoon was adjudged the best Champion NCO and was presented a Self -Loading Rifle (SLR) by Lt. Colonel Ronald Pope, the GDF 1st Chief of Staff.

On February 2, 1970, the 1st Standard Officers Course commenced; it was conducted by 2nd Lieutenant Victor Wilson, the Officer in Command was Capt. Oscar D. Pollard. The course concluded in July. On July 22, 1970, six cadets received their commissions.

In August 1970, the 2nd Standard Officers Course commenced. It was conducted by 2nd Lieutenant Victor Wilson. The Officer in Command was Capt. Asad Ishoof. The course concluded in January 1971. Also in 1971 Major Carl Morgan took over the command of Training Wing.

In February 1971, the 1st Junior Staff Course for Officers (subalterns) commenced under the leadership of Capt. Harry B. Hinds, and concluded in March 1971.

In April 1971 the 1st Junior Command and Tactics Course for Officers was conducted by Lt. Victor Wilson and concluded on May 6, 1971.

In August 1971, the Escape and Evasion course at Tacama Battle School was conducted under the leadership of Maj. Carl Morgan and Capt. Marcus Munroe, for the duration of one week.

In 1972, the Training Wing was renamed the Training Corps with three Divisions:

1) Recruit Division - Headed by Lt. Compton Hartley Liverpool
2) Skills Division – Headed by NCO's Orville Nedd and Dennis Stewart
3) Tactical Division (Jungle Warfare) Headed by – NCO's Albert Benjamin and Pelham Van Cooten.

In 1972 Major David Granger was appointed Commanding Officer of Training Corps.

In 1974 Major Fairbairn Liverpool was appointed Commanding Officer of Training Corps.

In May 1978, the Internal Security School of Internal Security Studies (ISS ISS) was established and headed by Major Compton Hartley Liverpool.

In September 1978 The GDF Officer School was built and named Colonel Ulric Pilgrim Officer Cadet School.

In October 1978 Major Compton Hartley Liverpool was appointed Commanding Officer of Training Corps; taking over the Command from Lieutenant Colonel Fairbairn Liverpool.

In November 1978 Lieutenant Colonel Watson Joseph was appointed Commanding Officer of Training Corps.

In March 1981 Major Compton Hartley Liverpool was appointed Commanding Officer of Training Corps; taking over the Command from Lieutenant Colonel Watson Joseph.

In July 1981 Major Perry Foo was appointed Commanding Officer of Training Corps; taking over the Command from Major Compton Hartley Liverpool.

In 1982, The Tacama Battle School in the Berbice Savannahs formally known as Camp Haywood was renamed Col. John Clarke Military School, and home of the Basic Recruit Courses (BRC).

In 1987, The Colonel Cecil Martindale Command and Staff School was established. Courses offered included: Senior Command and Staff Course (SCSC), Junior Command and Staff Course

(JCSC), Senior Leader Course (SLC), Force Instructors Training (FIT), and Force Method of Instruction (FMOI).

In 1998, The Jungle Training School was opened at Mokouria; Essequibo located 20 miles up the Essequibo River on a 1,400 acre site. It was constructed in 1941 as a United States Naval Air Station; upon an agreement with Great Britain under the Destroyer Base agreement of September 2, 1941. The site was decommissioned by the U.S. Government in September 1944.

On November 20, 2009, it was renamed, Colonel Robert Mitchell Jungle and Amphibious School.

Friday, November 18, 2005, The Guyana Defence Force (GDF), as part of its 40th Anniversary activities, re-dedicated two schools at Base Camp Stephenson in honour of the contribution of Colonels Desmond Roberts and Carl Morgan to the army.

The former Non-Commissioned Officers' Skills School was renamed the Colonel Desmond Roberts Skilled School (Symmetry and Accuracy). Training at the school focuses around the Platoon Commander Course (PCC), Skill-at-Arms Course (SAA), Skilled -at-Arms Instructors Course (SAAIC), Drill Course (DC), and Drill Instructors course (DIC).

The Non-Commissioned Tactics School was renamed the Colonel Carl Morgan School. Courses are conducted for Sergeants to be promoted to Platoon Sergeants (PSC), Section Commanders Course (SCC), and Junior Leader Course (JLC) for Lance Corporals and Privates.

The Training Corps remains active and vibrant.

Chapter 21

Guyana Defence Force Women's Army Corps (WAC's)

The establishment of the Guyana Defence Force Women's Army Corps (WAC) in February 1967, was a direct result of Venezuela's seizure of Ankoko Island in the Cuyuni River in October 1966.

After Guyana's Independence on May 26, 1966, the GDF which was formed in November 1965, it had barely established its first battalion of fewer than 500 men, when it was forced to deploy troops to Eteringbang on the country's western frontier to confront Venezuela's aggression. The sudden removal of a large number of men from such a small force had severely impacted the operations of the GDF; as some recruits were still undergoing basic training. Others were deployed along the coastland, which, only two years earlier in 1964, had been the scene of ethnic strife; creating huge manpower problems. Soldiers had to be found quickly to secure the borders and others had to take their place in the camps. The GDF's solution was to recruit women.

On January 30, 1967 Captain Joan Granger and Officer Cadets Brenda Aaron, Clarissa Hookumchand and Hyacinth King were of the First Company of the Women's Volunteer

Corps, who underwent a special one-week orientation course at Base Atkinson Field, now Base Camp Stephenson, Timehri.

On Sunday February 6, 1967 they were joined by 60 other women who were recruited, and then underwent five weeks of training in drill, field-craft, signals, skill-at-arms, shooting and physical fitness at Base Atkinson Field.

The course was divided into three squads; under instructors Major Cecil E. Martindale, Regimental Sergeant Major (RSM)) WO1 Ronald Sargeant, a British citizen, and three Non Commissioned Officers (NCO's), Sgt. Willian Oliver of the 3rd UK Parachute Regiment, Sgt. Compton Hartley Liverpool, and Corporal Mohamed Kahleel. The 60 female recruits were formally inducted into the GDF at a 'Passing Out/Graduation' parade held on March 12 at the Thomas Lands Base Camp (now Camp Ayanganna) in Georgetown, and inspected by Mrs. Winifred Gaskin, then Minister of Education.

The squad trained by Sgt. Liverpool was adjudged the best squad at the 'Passing Out' parade with WAC Gwen Davis being adjudged the 'Best Recruit'. On that day they created history in South America as the only women's army in the region.

The day after their 'passing out' parade, the women were all sent back home. Thereafter, they were to be called up once annually or only when required, as in any military reserve.

Initially, women soldiers were required to enlist in the 2nd Battalion (the GDF reserve) only for three (3) years and training was geared to prepare them for their specific role.

Women were paid, trained and treated as temporary reservists who could be disembodied, or have their full time service stopped at any time if their post became redundant, or they ceased to fulfill employment standards.

In May 1967, W/Lt. Brenda Aaron and 30 WAC members were activated into the regular army and worked in departments where their skills were required, such as, clerks, cooks, typists, drivers, radio and telephone operators, and storekeepers, Military Police (MP), Medical Corps and Intelligence Corps.

On September 26, 1969, only one month after the Surinamese/New River border conflict, the second batch and much larger than the first batch of women soldiers joined the GDF and, from that time, they were given combat training.

In 1975, An all women ceremonial guard-of-honor greeted Prime Minister Sirimavo Bandaranaike of Sri Lanka (formerly Ceylon) upon her arrival at the then Timehri Airport during her state visit to Guyana. Major Brenda Aaron was Officer in charge of the parade, and the 'Colour Party' comprised of Lt. Cheryl Pickering, Sgt. Lorraine Glasgow, Cpl. Lynette Smith and Cpl. Marva Nedd. Lt. Pickering, color ensign, performed that most sacred military ritual of carrying the Force Colour.

In addition, an all women detachments participated in the ceremonial 'Changing of the Guard' at Guyana House - the President's residence - and Remembrance Day parades.

In 1976 – May 16, the doors to regular officer training in Guyana were opened when eight women four civilians and four soldiers - were admitted to the Standard Officers Course (SOC) which all cadets must complete before being commissioned as officers.

On June 15 1976, The WAC Force was strengthened by the addition of a new batch of recruits.

Post 1976, the WAC Force grew and among the Corps, many firsts were achieved.

Three (3) members from this first batch of February 1967 - Margaret 'Maggie' Arthur, Angie Duncan and Janice Jordan became the first WAC's to achieve the rank of Warrant Officer (WO) II. Shortly thereafter, Janice Jordan became the first female WO I.

1977 – Ms. Beverly Drake and Cheryl Pickering became the first female fixed wing pilots in the Nation.

1992 – W/Sergeant Beverly 'Thriller' Somerset who joined the GDF in June 1976 was the first female soldier to climb Mount Ayanganna to its 6,700 feet peak.

2004 – W/Lt. Samantha Chung became the first female officer to climb Mount Ayanganna.

2005 - W/Lieutenant Christine Bradford became the first female officer to climb Mount Ayanganna 'to hoist the golden arrowhead'.

2009 - W/Private Melika Scotland earned the parachute badge becoming the first female paratrooper in the GDF.

December 2014, Lance Corporal Indrani Lyte became the second female paratrooper in the GDF.

2010 - October 31, W/ Lt. Nellon McKenzie led a patrol of female soldiers that successfully completed OPERATION ARROWHEAD hoisting the Golden Arrowhead and the Guyana Defence Force Flag atop Mt. Ayanganna. The event heralded the official commencement of the Force's 45th Anniversary celebrations.

2012 – January 2012, Windee Algernon was promoted to become the first female Colonel in the GDF.

2012 – W/Lieutenant Cadogan was honoured for being the first female officer to participate in the platoon commanders' course, which was previously reserved exclusively for male soldiers.

Starting with 64 recruits in 1967, the Women's Army Corps reached its greatest strength of 268 in 1977. It fell to 247 in 1987 and thereafter, declined slowly. There were 190 women soldiers serving in the GDF in 1997 and 260 at the start of 2002.

The Maritime Corps

GUYANA MARINE WING

January 9, 1967 The Marine Wing was established with 1 Officer & 22 Ranks, and by 1977 it had grown to 8 Officers & 400 Ranks.

The Unit was originally located at Thomas Lands now Camp Ayanganna and was accommodated in close proximity to the gymnasium, and headed by Lieutenant (Lt.) Harry B. Hinds before the recruitment and appointment of Lt. Joseph Skeete as the unit Commanding Officer. In 1969, Lt. Joseph Skeete suffered a devastating injury while swimming at Red Water Creek in Atkinson Field. Shortly thereafter, Capt. Harry B. Hinds was selected to command the Marine Wing.

The Marine Wing main base is located at Ruimveldt (now known as Col. Harry Basil Hinds Coast Guard HQ) on the East Bank of Demerara with four (4) additional bases, one at Benab /63 Beach Corentyne, and three in the North West District: Morawhanna, Port Kaituma, and Makouria.

1967 – The Marine Wing acquired four (4) boats a/k/a "IRON BOATS" made by Sprostons of Lombard Street, Charlestown and named after dangerous snakes – COMOUDI, LABARIA, RATTLER, HYMERALLY.

Crew : 1 Corporal and 8 men.

1969 – Marine Wing received three (3) 40 feet River Patrol launches from the Vosper Boat Company of Portsmouth, England – JAGUAR, OCELOT, MORGAY that were the first self- contained (cooking and lodging) vessels acquired by the Marine Wing. The MORGAY was destroyed by FIRE in the late 1970's and the remaining two (2) were decommissioned in the early 1990.

1970 - Name changed to Maritime Command.

1975 – The trawler EKEREKU which was previously used for fishing was converted into a patrol craft.

1976 – The PECCARI (DFS 1010), the 1st fast patrol boat (FPB [103 feet]) was acquired from England and arrived in Georgetown in 1977 after several weeks in crossing the Atlantic. It was decommissioned in 1991 after being out of service for 5 years (1986). A crew of seven (7) and twenty two (22) departed Guyana for England for training and sailing the ship to Guyana.

1977 – Two (2) South Korean fishing vessels, Kwangh Moyand 302 & Kwang 309 were seized for illegal fishing in Guyana waters off Suriname. The Captain of both vessels Jung Rim Kim & Chong Woon Lee were detained and brought to Georgetown for trial.

Note: Several fishing vessels (trawlers) that were apprehended on fishery protection patrols were seized by the court. THE MAKANDRA II, a fishing trawler was given to the Maritime Corps (1980's) and re-named MAIPURI (DF107) and converted to a patrol vessel. It was later sold to a private citizen

1979 – Two (2) 65ft Fast Attack Crafts (FAC) were acquired from North Korea (Peoples Democratic Republic of Korea) and used for Fisheries Protection Patrols.

Also in 1979, six (6) "Inshore Patrol Boats" were acquired from East Germany (German Democratic Republic). 3 of the 6 were known as GRASSHOPPERS (DF1013, DF1014, DF1015); the remaining three were named HASSA, HOURI, PIRAI.

1980 – Name changed to Maritime Corps.

1990 –Maritime Corps renamed Coast Guard with the passing of the Defence (Amendment)Act of 1990

2001 – May, Four (4) 44ft patrol vessels were obtained from the United States – BARACUDA, PERAI, TIRAPUKU, HYMARA. CREW: 1 Coxswain, 1 Engineer and 2 crewmembers.

2001 – The Coast Guard acquired a Presidential Craft.

2001 – May The Coast Guard acquired the 165ft patrol vessel, the GDFS ESSEQUIBO formerly the HMS ORWELL (Minesweeper) from the United Kingdom.

Crew: 9 Officers and 45 Ratings.

2009 – The MV HYMARALLI – an Inceptor was acquired from the U.S.A. Crew: 1 operator & 2 Ratings.

2009 – Nov 20 – Coast Guard HQ renamed Harry Hinds.

2014 – March – The USA 'gifted' three (3) Metal Shark Boats to the GDF. The Metal Sharks can be used for the provision of services and functions such as containment, restriction of waterways, seizure of coastal force, tactical situation, insertion, extraction, board and bank search, waterborne ambush and night movement.

In addition, the newly acquired "Sharks" can be used to carry out military assaults, blocking action, convoy support, high value transit protection and other functions.

The boats which are the first U.S made boats to be used by the GDF Coast Guard are being regarded as valuable assets being added to its marine fleet. The boats are equipped with special communications equipment to aid in the timely sharing of information and coordination between the vessels on the water and personnel on land and in the air.

Guyana Defence Force (GDF) Air Wing

In 1967 The Guyana Defence Force Air Wing was formed upon the acquisition of a Helio-Courier Aircraft from the United States of America. It was flown by Major Neil Pullen of the British Army; he was seconded to the GDF as Officer Commanding the Training Wing (Infantry). It was A Helio-Courier single engine Short Take Off and Landing (STOL) aircraft; nicknamed Rudolph by the soldiers because of its bright red nose. "Rudolph" quickly became beloved by soldiers stationed in remote jungle locations, because its large cabin could transport an enormous amount of rations, and its STOL performance could deliver the cargo to rudimentary or even incomplete landing strips. Over a period of time, the Guyana Defence Force fleet of aircraft had increased to include four twin engines Islanders, a Sky Van and eight assorted helicopters.

In 1973 The Air Wing was renamed the GDF Air Command.

On November 8th, 2013, The Air Corps was renamed Air Station London

Between 1973 and 1990 when I retired from the GDF, the Air Command had acquired 14 fixed wing aircrafts and 11 helicopters.

7 Britte Norman Islander (High Wing Skyvan [1975-2001]) from the UK.
3 Helio Super Courier (Patrol [1967-1971]) from the USA.
1 Beechcraft Super King (Transport [1975-1992]) from the USA
1 Cessna 182 (Liaison [1982-1994]) from the USA.
1 Cessna 206 (Transport / Patrol [1975-1995]) from the USA
1 Embraer – EMB110 – Bandeirante (Transport [1984-1994]) Brazil

Helicopters:

3 Bell 212 (1976 – 1994) from the USA.
1 Bell 412

185

2 Bell 206

3 MI-8 (1985-1991) from Russia

2 Aerospatiale Aloutee (1975 – 1982) France

Both Aloutee crashed - 1976 -Major Anthony Mekdeci crashed (8R GEM) at LOO CREEK close to the Linden Highway.

Capt. Phillip Payne and Ensign Jarvis crashed in the Rupununi Savannah at Mar Kanata

On January 18 1981 - A short SC.7 Skyvan (8R-GFF) crashed – 4 Fatalities. Robert Roberts (vanished). His name was placed on Sky Van 8R-GRR in his memory.

On November 8, 2013, The Air Corps was re- named Air Station London.

Names of Female Pilots:

Cheryl Pickering Moore – First female military pilot in the GDF

Beverly Christiani Drake-Johnson – First commercial pilot in Guyana

Barbara Adams - First female helicopter pilot in GDF

Names of Male Pilots:

Anthony Mekdeci, Phillip Payne, Egbert 'Eggy' Fields, Robert Roberts, Chris Cameron, Gerry Gouveia, Jeff Roman, Lloyd Nurse, Claude St. Romaine, Williet Lord, Peter DaSilva, David Totaram (Bell 412 Helicopter), Owen Sandiford (Helicopter), Derek Poole (Helicopter), Miles Williams, Larry London ; Andre Budhan, Rohan Sharma, Francis Vieira.

1981 - January 18 – Short SC.7 Skyvan (8R-GFF) crashed – 4 Fatalities. Robert Roberts (vanished). His name was placed on the nose of Sky Van 8R-GRR in honour of his memory.

1986 – December 15 – Britten Norman Islander (8R –GES) crashed. No fatalities.

2001 – January 6 – Britten Norman BN -2A-2 Islander (8R – GFN) crashed – 3 fatalities.

2007 – April 25 – Rohan Sharma while flying for Air Service Limited (ASA) crashed into the Yurubarrow Mountain before reaching Kopinang, Potaro/Siparuni.

Chapter 22

The Engineer Command

The Pioneer Platoon of the Engineer Command

The Pioneer Platoon of the Engineer Command was established in April 1967. The Office in Command was Lieutenant Oscar Pollard; the Platoon Sargent was Sargent Ulric Sutton. The Pioneer Platoon was also comprised of twenty four Other Ranks. The Pioneer Platoon was stationed at Base Atkinson Field. The first task, undertaken by the Pioneer Platoon was the construction of an ammunition dump at Tacama.

The Pioneer Platoon was also involved in the construction of airstrips at Eteringbang and Kurutoka in the Cuyuni River area.

In December 1968 2nd Lieutenant Haydock West, returned from Sandhurst Officer Cadet School with an Engineering Degree. He was appointed Officer Commanding the Pioneer Platoon; he replaced Lieutenant Oscar Pollard. Further, in mid-1968 carpenters, masons, joiners, plumbers and electricians, were recruited into the GDF. With this recruitment, the construction company of the Engineer Command was established. Captain Hubert Franklin was appointed Officer Commanding the Construction Company.

The Construction Company built a number of buildings at the GDF farm at Garden of Eden on the East Bank, Demerara. They are the Administration building, a Barrack Room, four chicken pens, a plucking house, and a piggery where the pigs are bred and raised. Once, completed they fenced the farm at Garden of Eden.

In 1969, Major Vernon Williams was appointed Commanding Officer of the Engineer Command. Subsequently, the Engineer Command; then established its Headquarters at the corner of New Market and Main Streets. This building was the residence on the former Chief of Staff of the Guyana Defence Force, Colonel Ronald Pope.

In 1970, the Construction Company began erecting the Medical Centre in Camp Ayanganna. When the project was completed, they had built a two level Medical Centre. The top level was a hospital with twenty-four beds; that accommodated male and female soldiers; the offices of doctors and nurses; as well as an examination room.

In addition, the Dispensary and the Dentistry of the Medical Centre were located on the lower level. Likewise, in 1971 the Engineer Command built a large concrete bond at Camp Ayanganna for the Ordinance Corps. Further, in 1971 Major Claude V. Bowen replaced Major Vernon Williams as Commanding Office of the Engineer Command.

In 1972, Major Clarence Gordon replaced Major Claude Bowen as Commanding Officer of the Engineer Command. In 1975 thirty soldiers of the Engineer Command were sent to Cuba for training. Accordingly, on their return six month later the Combat Engineers was formed. Major Hubert Humphrey was appointed Officer Commanding the Combat Engineers. Similarly, in 1975 the Engineer Command constructed a Base for 11 Infantry Battalion at Low Creek on the Soesdyke Linden Highway.

In 1973, a Company size unit of the Engineer Command was directly involved in the road construction of the Mazaruni Hydro-Electric Project where they operated heavy equipment.

In 1978 the Engineer Command constructed the Colonel Ulric Pilgrim Officer Cadet School at Camp Stephenson. In 1979, the Engineer Command elevated the Officer's Mess Hall in Camp Ayanganna; from a one level to a two level building. When the structure was completed, the top level was the dining room with a television room and a veranda. The lower level was the GDF bar and restrooms facilities.

In 1980, the 4 Engineer Command erected the All Ranks Club and Pavilion at Camp Ayanganna. Additionally, at Camp Ayanganna, they elevated the Sergeant's Mess Hall from one level to a two level building.

Later, in 1980 the Engineer Command assist in the development of 12 Infantry Battalion Base at Long Creek. They repaired the administrative building, built a new arms store, repaired the ordinance stores, constructed a kitchen mess hall complex, an All Ranks Club and erected a fence around the camp. In 1980, the Engineer Command constructed the GDF Air Corps Hangar and Air Corps Headquarters at Timerhi Airport.

In 1986, the Combat Engineers Commanded by Major Hubert Humphrey erected a steel bridge across the Barima River at Arakaka in Region number 1. The Engineer Command, in acceding to the dreams of the Leader, constructed houses at Melanie Damishana, and Vryheid Lust on East Coast Demerara.

Further, they constructed a housing scheme for the Senior NCO at the junction of Mandela Avenue and East Bank public road. Most importantly; they constructed the GDF Nursing Home in East Ruimveldt. The Construction Company, is currently being Commanded by Major Kennard Liverpool.

By 1987, Engineer Command constructed new accommodations, for soldiers at Camps Jaguar, Eteringbank, Kaikan and Lethem.

The Engineer Company continues to serve the GDF as a vibrant Command. The Commanding Officer is Lieutenant Colonel Lawrence Fraser, who replaced the Former Commander, Lieutenant Colonel Gary Beaton.

The Agriculture Corps

The Agriculture Corps of the GDF was established in 1969, the Officer in Command was Lieutenant Neville Henry. He had a staff of ten that comprised of one Sargent and nine Other Ranks. The Agriculture Corps established a farm at Garden of Eden on the East Bank, Demerara. Originally, the farm had ten milch cows; kept for milking; six sows and one chicken pen, 75 feet by 25 feet in size.

In 1970, the Engineer Command constructed an Administrative building, a Barrack room, a plucking house and four additional chicken pens. Three pens were for broiler chickens and one for layers. The built a piggery and they fenced the farm. Furthermore, in 1970 Sergeant Francis Chichester of 2 Company was transferred to Agriculture Corps as Second in Command. The Agriculture Corps planted green vegetables on seven acres of land. The planted bok choy, mustard, poi callaloo, bora, ochra, squash and pumpkins.

In 1971, Lieutenant Neville Henry, left for the United States of America, to attend the Tuskegee Agricultural Institute. While he was in Tuskegee, Lieutenant Neville Henry was promoted to the rank of Captain. On his return, the Agriculture Corps established a twenty five acres rice farm at Onverwagt on the Abary River. They established a twenty five acres farm at Butenabu, Mahaicony River, where they cultivated rice and ground provisions.

In 1972 they established a farm at Vergenoegen on the East Bank Essequibo River. At this farm they cultivated citrus and ground provisions.

In 1973 they dug four ponds; three for rearing tilapia fish and one for turtles. The turtles were supplied by Deputy Prime Minister Dr. Ptolemy Reid.

In 1974 the GDF was self-sufficient in eggs. Chicken was in adequate supply, with approximately 1,000 birds being slaughtered in a week. There were also over 150 turtles and a duck brood at the farm. Also in 1974, the Agriculture Corps had won many prizes at the National Agricultural Exhibition at Sophia. Further, in December 1974, Sergeant Francis Chichester, was promoted to the rank of Warrant Officer 2.

At Garden of Eden, production of greens and vegetables averaged over 1,700 pounds per month. There was also an extensive cultivation of corn, and the pig herd which was initially started with six sows had grown to over 150 pigs by 1975.

In 1975, Warrant Officer 2 Francis Chichester and Captain Neville Henry left for the United States of America, to attend the Tuskegee Agricultural College. Major Rohan Seeapaul was appointed Commanding Officer of the Agriculture Corps. While at Tuskegee Agricultural College, Warrant Officer 2 Chichester was commissioned with the rank of Lieutenant, and Captain Henry was promoted to the rank of Major.

In 1976, Lieutenant Chichester returned to Guyana and took over command of the Agriculture Corp from Major Seeapaul; then Major Seeapaul left to attend a military course in Brazil.

In 1977, Major Henry returned to Guyana and he was seconded to the Guyana National Service as the Agriculture Officer. Lieutenant Chichester continued as Commanding Officer until 1980. During this period he was promoted to the rank of Captain.

In 1980, Major Calvin Clarke was appointed Commanding Officer of the Agriculture Corps and Captain Chichester remained as second in Command. At the time of writing, and for the last twenty three years the Agriculture has deteriorated to the extent that they no longer produce agriculture crops. The farm only produces eggs, chickens and pork.

Ordnance (Five Service Support) Battalion

Five Service Support Battalion

The Ordnance Corps is the Supply Corps of the GDF. It is one of the many Quartering or Logistic Services of which their tasks are interdependent.

The roles and subsequent tasks of the unit have not changed significantly over the years. The earliest roles were:

A. **Supply.**

The supply of all commodities included under the generic heading of Ordnance Materiel (combat supplies, ordnance stores, vehicles) in order to satisfy the operational, training and routine peacetime needs of the Army wherever it is stationed.

B. **Inspection and Repairs.**

(1) Inspection, proof and repair of arms and ammunition and the investigation of accidents, losses and defects.

(2) Quality surveillance of ration and petroleum products.

(3) Repair of general stores such as tentage, clothing and some furniture.

C. **Specialist Services**.

A variety of functions connected with the supply role are also carried out by Ordnance Corps under operational conditions, but in peace time many are carried out by contractors. Some of these roles are no longer carried out by the unit but are done by contractors on a permanent basis. These specialist services are:

(1) Local procurement.

(2) Materials production Centre capable of producing the Army's requirement for printed material such as training aids, pamphlets, programmes, invitations, booklets as well as plaques, GDF embossed key purses, wallets etc.

(3) Laundry.

(4) Tailoring.

(5) Butchery.

(6) Wood Products Centre capable of producing the Force's need for office furniture, beds, kit boxes and minor wood products.

(7) Office Equipment Repairs Centre capable of servicing and effecting minor repairs to all office equipment and accounting machines.

ORGANISATION

To achieve its role the Corps is equipped to manage stores and workshop and to provide staff for the entire 'Quartering' system of the Force. The Corps in earlier times was organised for supply and training as follows:

Supply Organisation.

Central Control The CO Ord Corps a Major was responsible to the Force Commander through the Quartermaster General (QMG) who was a Grade One Staff Officer in the Force Headquarters, for the efficient conduct of the supply, inspection and repair, and specialists tasks.

Base Control CO Ord had a subordinate commander OC Ord Company who was responsible for base storage and supply. In this case the Base is located at Camp Stephenson, which because of its geographical location catered for the supply of the base itself; as well as highway locations and north and south interior sectors. This base also catered for supply of Tacama Battle School.

Training Organisation HQ Ord Corps: Is responsible for the training of all storekeepers, arms store men, armourers and tailors. Band two and three courses are equivalent to the NCOs TAC 1 and 2 respectively while Band 4 produces the Quarter Master Warrant Officer or Junior Quartermaster.

OPERATIONS AND TRAINING

The unit has lent very valuable and invaluable support to all operations and training activities that the Force has been involved in.

The unit played a support role in the operation conducted in the New River Triangle in August of 1969 and the one following the Rupununi Uprising in 1969. It also supported Operations PLEXUS, DRAGNET, and ARROWHEAD among others.

The Corps has played and continues to play a support role in all training exercises conducted by the Force including IRONWEED, GREENHEART and those conducted by units in the Force.

LEADERSHIP OF THE CORPS

a. Unit Commanders and Former Commanders of the unit included Major Daniel Debbington, a British citizen, Maj. Claude Graham, Major Richardson, Capt. Forbes, Maj. Patrick Smith, Maj. Walter Davis, Lt. Col. Randolph Storm, Lt. Col T. Ross, and Lt. Col. N. Hussain.

b. Unit Regimental Quartermasters. Former RQMS' of the Corps included WO2 Perks, a British citizen, Capt. Andrew Hartley, WO2 Milton Dalgetty, WO2 B. Dehnert, SSGT Rodney E, and WO2 J. Peters.

Chapter 23

The first two Guyanese at the United States Military Academy, West Point, NY

1969 Guyanese - West Point Appointment

In 1968, the United States Government as part of its Foreign Aid assistance to the Government of Guyana, offered scholarships for two (2) of its high school students for a four (4) year period, each, to attend the prestigious United States Military Academy (USMA) at West Point, NY (50 miles north of NY City).

October 1968, the headmaster at Queens College (QC), Doodnauth Hetram, summoned selected students to his 3rd floor office to advise them of the unique opportunity available to attend USMA and further advised them that they would have to compete in a scholarship competition for selections. Those and many more applied for consideration.

The candidates were engaged in several rounds of preliminary interviews with officials from the Guyana and U.S. Government. The panel for the in-country stage of the selections process included:

Col. Clarence Price, Chief Of Staff (COS) of the Guyana Defence Force

Oscar Agard, Permanent Secretary, Ministry of Education

Oscar Henry, Permanent Secretary to the Prime Minister's Office

William Mateer, U.S. Embassy

Paul Kattenburg, Former Deputy Chief of U.S. Mission to Guyana.

The six candidates, who emerged from the panel interviews, were invited to submit written applications to USMA. Subsequently, three of them received personal notification letters dated January 15, 1969 from U.S. Army Major General Kenneth G. Wickham, Adjutant General in Washington, D.C. advising them of their nomination for further consideration to be admitted to USMA on July 1, 1969 from the Government of Guyana. In addition, the letter outlined that an examination will be required and such examination will be conducted at 08:30 hours on March 1, 1969 at the College Entrance Examination Board Center at Fountain A.M.E. School in Georgetown.

Thereafter, the headmaster at QC, Doodnaught Hetram summoned two of the final three candidates, separately, to announce and congratulate them of their acceptance and admission into the United States Military Academy (USMA) at West Point, New York. Thus Conrad Taylor and Chaitram Singh became the 1st two Guyanese to be accepted at the United States Military Academy.

June 28, 1969, the 'student agreement' was signed and both students departed Guyana for four (4) years of rigorous training above the Hudson River at West Point, NY.

Wednesday June 6, 1973 saw Conrad Taylor and Chaitram Singh standing tall in the honoured 'Long Gray Line' after successfully completing the four (4) years of an intense mix of academic, military and physical requirements. Each earned a Bachelor's of Science degree in Engineering and the coveted Parachute Wing.

Upon their return home separately in June and July 1973, Conrad and Chaitram met with the Chief of Staff of the Guyana Defence Force (GDF), Brigadier General Clarence Price. He was a Colonel, when he was part of the early screening of Guyanese scholarship candidates to West Point, NY. During that meeting, the General summarily dismissed their four (4) years at West Point as "Irrelevant to the GDF mission."

The General proceeded to inform them that they would enter the GDF as Officer Cadets and be 'considered' for commission only after successful completion of the Army's (GDF) local nine (9) month officer training course.

With no other choice, subsequent to their meeting with General Price, they officially reported for duty in August 1973 at Camp Ayanganna (the former Thomas Lands) headquarters in Georgetown as Officer Cadets. There, they met with Major Joe Singh, Officer responsible for Operations and Training, who confirmed to them that they would be undergoing nine (9) months of military training as Brigadier Price required. Further, Major Singh informed them, without explanation, of plans to send them the following day to the Battle School at Tacama located on the Berbice River.

After an overnight stay in a mosquito infested room at Camp Ayanganna, they traveled to Base Camp Timehri the following morning, where they reported to Camp Commander, Major Fairbairn Liverpool. That meeting was a prelude of things to come when Major Liverpool, irked by their failure to salute him, severely admonished them.

Shortly thereafter, they boarded an army transport aircraft for the Tacama Battle School, without any explanation from Major Fairbairn Liverpool either. Upon arrival at Tacama, the school commander Lieutenant (Lt.) Compton Ross greeted them in a hostile, disrespectful and unprofessional manner. Ross refused to talk to Taylor and Singh (both former classmates of his at QC), other than to inform them about their being in a force walk the next day. His subsequent actions became further detestable (execrable), when both 'cadets' informed him they will NOT participate in any hiking, drilling or other activity at Camp Tacama. Lt. Ross's response was to reach for his side arm and unload a round (bullet) from its chamber before reloading the pistol in a deliberate act of intimidation.

Lt. Ross, after communication with Camp Ayanganna in Georgetown, placed them under house arrest. They were flown back to Base Camp Timehri later on the following day accompanied by Lt. Ross. Upon arrival, they were locked up in the jail there. Lieutenant George Maynard, the evening Orderly Officer, later handcuffed them to each other for a short trip. Under the cover of darkness, he took them to the Timehri Officer's Quarters where they were paraded, mocked, and ridiculed before their reporting to the Training Corps the following day.

Upon their arrival at the Training Corps, they learned that the requirement to attend the nine (9) month 1973 GDF Officer Cadet Training Course had been waived and their training period was reduced to three (3) months.

After successfully completing the three (3) month course, they were assigned to the Engineering Command under Colonel Williams at the rank of 'Officer Cadets.' It wasn't until December 1973 when they were promoted to the rank of second (2nd) Lieutenant's (subaltern's).

Both Taylor and Singh petitioned The Guyana Government in 1974 to be released from the GDF. It released 2nd Lt Chaitram Singh, first, to become a high school teacher. A few months later, in November 1974, the Government released 2nd Lt, Conrad Taylor to become an engineer at the Guyana Electricity

Corporation. It took a face-to-face appeal to Prime Minister Burnham for that to happen. Conrad Taylor followed his path to Freedom, when he immigrated to the United States in January 1977. Chaitram Singh did the same in late 1977.

1973 Upper Mazaruni Hydro-Electric Project

The Upper Mazaruni District is located in the west-central part of Guyana, bordering Venezuela and Brazil and is part of the Guiana Shield, recognized as one of the most ancient and vulnerable ecosystems on earth.

During the 1973 elections campaign, Prime Minister Forbes Linden Sampson Burnham announced an ambitious plan stating his administration intended to develop a large hydro-electric power complex in the Upper Mazaruni River region aimed at powering an aluminum smelter to be built at Linden, formerly known as McKenzie. At that time, Guyana was spending an inordinate amount (more than 25 percent) of its Gross Domestic Product on fuel imports.

In 1974, PM Burnham sought the assistance of United Nations Development Program (UNDP) which provided a grant to enable a major hydro-electric survey in the country. The UNDP appointed the World Bank as the executing agency and a Montreal Engineering Company was contracted as the consulting firm. The survey included hydro resource feasibility studies of a limited number of sites.

In 1975, a full scale feasibility study of the area was carried out. Through this survey, the established plan was to harness the Kumarau Falls on the Kurupung River which would provide enough power to smelt the bauxite at McKenzie/Linden. Kamarau Falls is approximately 35 miles (as the crow flies) North by east (NbE [11degrees]) from Imbaimadai and 60 miles Northeast by east(NEbE [56 degrees]) from Paruima Mission.

Also, in 1975, the Government began to inform the Akawaio and Aracuna Amerindian communities of Paruima, Waramadong, Kamarang, Kako, Jawalla, Phillipai, Chinowieng and Imbaimadai of the plan for the construction of the dam and the creation of a reservoir for the hydro-electric project. In March 1975, the Toshaos (captains) of the Akawaio and Arekuna villages in the region were hurriedly called to Georgetown to meet with the Minister of Energy and Natural Resources, Hubert Jack. At the meeting, Mr. Jack informed them, that the villages in their community would be flooded as part of the reservoir and that the government wanted their cooperation in the resettlement of the 4,000+ residents.

There were disagreements among the the Toshaos (Captains) on the resettlement issue. In addition, Mr. Jack never gave them a specific area where they will be resettled and he went on to inform those who had objected to this plan, that the decision to flood their villages was final and could not be changed. He also tried to convince them that the hydro project would give the Amerindians of the area an opportunity to contribute to the development of Guyana.

Early in 1976, the Government established the Upper Mazaruni Development Authority to administer the installation of the Upper Mazaruni Hydro-Electric Project and the aluminum smelter at Mckenzie/Linden. Later that year, the Government contracted the large Swiss company, Alusuisse, to undertake a feasibility study for the construction of the modern primary aluminum smelter at Linden. At the same time, Sweco, a Swedish consulting group, was contracted with World Bank assistance to conduct a feasibility study for the establishment of the Upper Mazaruni Diversion Scheme, including the building of the dam across the river. Both studies, completed during 1977, formed the basis for discussion between representatives of the Government of Guyana and multilateral financing agencies including the World Bank. These studies established the technical feasibility of the project. The overall plan for the development of the hydro power project involved the construction of a dam at 'The Sands' Landing on the Upper Mazaruni River located close to Oranapai / Sipariparu.

In addition, to be constructed was a headrace tunnel (the tunnel would takes water from connecting channels and convey it to the fore bay or directly to the penstock /optimum option) about 6.5 miles long through rock for a high perpetual/ uninterrupted drop leading to an underground powerhouse with accommodation for turbine generators with double-circuit transmission line, about 225 miles long from the powerhouse to McKenzie/ Linden where it would enter the national grid. Moreover, plans also included additional hinterland road construction, designed to support the proposed Upper Mazaruni Hydro-power project and to open new lines of transport beginning in Mahdia to Annai, Rupununi, which involved the GDF Engineer Corps.

Additionally, the building of the main access road included the use of the all-weather laterite surface for 190+ miles in length, from Itaballi located on the Essequibo River about 5 miles North of Rockstone. Rockstone is located 20+ miles West (270o) after crossing the Demerara River from McKenzie/Linden.

Opposition from the Amerindians

The Amerindians in the region when informed of the Government plan project by their Captains opposed the project primarily because of the proposed flooding of the area and their displacement which would have destroyed their way of life.

Venezuela informed

By the end of 1977, the blue-print for the huge multi-billion dollar hydro-electric project was ready. The drawings and two copies of the feasibility studies done by Sweco were forwarded to the Venezuelan Government which, according to the Guyana Government, did not object to the establishment of the project in that area, even though a part of Venezuelan territory was expected to be flooded on the completion of the scheme. The Guyana Government anticipated, too, that Venezuela would purchase excess energy generated by the hydro-electric turbines.

The Government also submitted an application to the World Bank for financing the project. In the meantime, it had begun to implement the scheme and by 1978 more than US$25 M was already spent from its own resources for starting the construction of the access road.

During the visit of Venezuela's President Carlos Andres Perez in October 1978 to Guyana, the project was fully discussed. At his press conference on 20 October 1978 at the end of his visit, Perez expressed Venezuela's general support for the project by declaring:

"Venezuela has decided to study the possibility of linking the present and future systems of the two countries and purchasing electricity from Guyana on the completion of the hydro-project. . . We will give all we can to help develop this complex."

Venezuela's opposition to the project

Shortly after the inauguration of Venezuelan President Luis Herrera Campins in 1979, Guyana's Minister of Energy and Mines, Hubert Jack, informed Venezuela's Foreign Minister Dr. José Alberto Velasco Zambrano in March 1979 of the progress of the project. The latter's response was that the Venezuelan Government needed time to study it.

The hydro-power project almost immediately after it started began to experience problems in obtaining international financial backing. Political groups in Venezuela, associated with the new Herrera Campins administration, began to oppose the establishment of the project in the area which they maintained was Venezuelan territory; and, no doubt, these objections caused international lending agencies to be hesitant in financing the project.

Up to the end of 1980 the project had not commenced because of the non-availability of international funding. While Guyana was awaiting a decision from the World Bank on its funding application, the *Caribbean Contact* of April 1981 wrote that Brazil was offering political support for the construction of the Mazaruni hydro dam, thus giving recognition of Guyana's sovereignty over Essequibo. Burnham, now President of Guyana, visited Venezuela at the beginning of April 1981 and the issue of Venezuela's cooperation in the implementation of the project was discussed. But events took a dramatic turn on the night of April 4, 1981, when the Venezuelan Government issued a communiqué stating that because of "Venezuela's claim on the Essequibo territory" it "asserted the rejection of Venezuela to the hydro-electric project of the upper Mazaruni." ***The communiqué also announced that Venezuela had no intention to renew the Protocol of Port of Spain which in 1970 had placed the border issue in abeyance for an initial period of 12 years.*** Burnham was very surprised by this Venezuelan action.

At a press conference on 8 April 1981, he stated that it was the first time Venezuela was expressing opposition to the Upper Mazaruni Hydro-Electric Project. He said the discussions in Venezuela were generally frank, cordial and open and "we sought to examine how economic and other forms of cooperation could be carried forward especially on the question of the Upper Mazaruni Hydro-Electric Project."

Border tensions escalated

The Venezuelan communiqué and Burnham's counter-statements obviously heated up the tensions between Guyana and Venezuela. In Caracas, the Venezuelan Foreign Affairs Minister, in re-asserting his country's claim to Guyana's Essequibo territory, stated on 10 April 1981: "In the specific case of the Upper Mazaruni Dam project, it should be made evident on the international level, that its construction, under the present conditions is unacceptable for Venezuela."

"Now that the Upper Mazaruni Hydro-Project is linked with border disputes and territorial claims, it has caused fear of danger to the Amerindian people, particularly the Akawaios who are settled within Upper Mazaruni. It is clear that the present Government is preparing to create refugees out of 4,000 Akawaio Amerindian people from the Upper Mazaruni region."

Venezuela's letter to the World Bank

Venezuelan hostility to the hydro-electric project moved significantly one step further on 8 June 1981 when the Foreign Minister, José Alberto Zambrano Velasco, wrote a letter to the President of the World Bank giving the multilateral institution an ultimatum to refrain from financing the Upper Mazaruni Hydro-Electric Project. ***While saying that Venezuela had never recognised the arbitral award of 1899,*** the letter further re-asserted Venezuela's claim to Guyana's territory, and alleged that "the objective pursued by Guyana with its Upper Mazaruni project was political". It also revealed that the Venezuelan Government would recognise "no right or legal situation which may be involved in the future by third states, international bodies or private corporations" based on the exercise of Guyana's sovereignty over the territory claimed by Venezuela.

Suspension of the project

With Venezuela maintaining its opposition to any World Bank financing, further work on the project was suspended and hundreds of workers were laid off. In a scathing attack on Venezuela, Burnham, in a speech on 23 February 1982 to mark Guyana's republic anniversary, referred to the Venezuelan Government's "attempt to block the World Bank's sponsorship of our hydro-power project; the pontifical statement that the hydro-power project is neither suitable for, or in the interest of Guyana; her lobbying of international agencies against investment in, or sponsorship, of projects in western Essequibo; protest to nations and corporations involved or to be involved in economic ventures along with the Government of Guyana in the area; a general campaign of economic aggression; interference in the internal affairs of Guyana..."

By 1984, the Guyana Government, after spending over a billion Guyana dollars on various aspects of the project, including employment costs, and failing to acquire international financing decided not to proceed any longer with the hydro project. As a result, the plan for the aluminium smelter was also shelved. This large expenditure of money on the Hydro Project left the Government facing a potential debt crisis forcing President Forbes Burnham to announce an austere program where he announced to the nation in May 1984 "that a nation should eat only what it produces" whereupon he imposed a ban on imported foods such as powdered milk, wheaten flour, split peas, and other canned goods. The food ban affected the dietary habits on the population, and also restricted training and border operations in the hinterlands of the country by members of the Defence Force; this opened the doors to smugglers who brought the banned items into the country from our neighbouring countries, Suriname, Venezuela and Brazil.

In addition, owing to the Nation's financial crunch, the Government placed a moratorium on the acquisition of Military logistical equipment from overseas such as weapons, ammunition, food, maintenance, materials, engineering and transportation vehicles that were in its inventory since 1966.

VENEZUELA's CLAIM TO THE COUNTY OF ESSEQUIBO, GUYANA

When Britain gained formal control over what is now Guyana in 1814, it also became involved in one of Latin America's most persistent border disputes. At the London Convention of 1814, the Dutch surrendered the United Colony of Demerara, Essequibo, and Berbice to the British. Although Spain still claimed the region, the Spanish did not contest the treaty because they were preoccupied with their own colonies' struggles for independence.

In 1840, the British Government commissioned and authorized Robert Hermann Schomburgk, a German surveyor, geographer and naturalist, to survey and mark out the boundaries of British Guiana (now Guyana). It was the intention of that Government, when the work was completed, to communicate to the Governments of Venezuela and Brazil the views of the British Government as to the true boundary of the colony, and then to settle by negotiation any details to which these Governments might take objection.

In carrying out this commission, Schomburgk personally investigated practically the whole of the country (west of the Essequibo) to the Barima and Amakura River (located immediate west of Morawhanna and Mora Passge of Guyana) that runs into the mouth of the River Orinoco, and points south of the Barima and Amakura River to the Cuyuni River, and westwards on the Cuyuni River beyond Makapa Hills and Eteringbang into the confluence of the Wenemu River where Ankoko Island is located. Schomburgk submitted his report with maps of his surveys that began with the showing British Guiana's western boundary with Venezuela at the mouth of the Orinoco River.

Venezuela protested, claiming the entire area west of the Essequibo River, approximately 50,000 of Guyana's 83,000 square mile territory or all of Barimi / Waini

(**Region 1** – Morawhanna, Mabaruma, Shell Beach, Port Kaituma, Matthews Ridge); Pomeroon / Supenaam

(**Region 2** – Charity, Anna Regina, Santa Rosa and Waramuri Mission, Lake Mainstay,); Essequibo Islands / West Demerara

(**Region 3** – Dartmouth, Danielstown, Henrietta, Reliance, Suddie, and all the islands including Tiger, Wakenaam, Leguan, Hog and Fort) ; Cuyuni / Mazaruni

(**Region 7** - Kamarang, Waramadan, Imbaimadai, Paruima, Kai-Kan); Potaro / Siparuni

(**Region 8** - Mahdia, Kaieteur Falls, Iwokrama); Upper Takutu / Upper Essequibo

(**Region 9** - All of the Rupununi from Apoteri south to Konashen, Karasabai, Annai, Karanambu, Lethem and Dadanawa.

Negotiations between Britain and Venezuela over the boundary began, but the two nations could reach no compromise. In 1850 both agreed NOT to occupy the disputed zone. The discovery of gold in the contested area in the late 1850s reignited the dispute. British settlers moved into the region and the British Guiana Mining Company was formed to mine the deposits. Over the years, Venezuela made repeated protests and proposed arbitration, but the British government was uninterested. Venezuela finally broke diplomatic relations with Britain in 1887 and appealed to the United States for help. The British at first rebuffed the United States government's suggestion of arbitration, but when President Grover Cleveland threatened to intervene according to the Monroe Doctrine, Britain agreed to let an international tribunal arbitrate the boundary in 1897.

For two years, the tribunal consisting of two Britons, two Americans, and a Russian studied the case. Their three-to-two decision, handed down in 1899, awarded over 90 percent of the disputed 89,000 square mile territory or 83,000 square miles to British Guiana. Venezuela received only the mouth of the Orinoco River and a short stretch of the Atlantic coastline just to the east. Although Venezuela was unhappy with the decision, a commission surveyed a new border in accordance with the award, and both sides accepted the boundary in 1905. The issue was considered settled for the next half - century.

In early 1952, Manganese Mines Management, Ltd; a subsidiary of Union Carbide Corporation of New York applied for a lease in Matthews Ridge (North-West District / Region 1) to mine extensive deposits of manganese ore. The production of columbite - tantalite on a small scale was begun in 1952. Between 1961-1966 over 1.7million metric tons of 40%+ Manganese (Mn) concentrate was produced. When the persistent sabre rattling by Venezuela resumed immediately after Guyana's independence on May 26, 1966. Union Carbide Corporation which also had manganese operations in Venezuela became **'risk averse'** (an investor who, when faced with two investments with a similar expected return [but different risks], will prefer the one with the lower risk)**,** prompting them to abandon their operations in Guyana, leaving among other property holdings, heavy equipment, railroad locomotives, river punts and a 40 mile / 64 Km railroad that ran between Matthews Ridge and Port Kaituma.

February 1966 - **The Geneva Agreement**. A two day **Geneva conference** on the Guyana-Venezuela border issue was held on February 16 & 17, 1966. The Guyana team at the conference, which joined up with the British delegation, included Burnham, Minister of State Shridath Ramphal and a group of advisers.

On the first day of the conference, opening speeches were delivered by the British Foreign Secretary Michael Stewart and Venezuelan Foreign Minister Ignacio Iribarren Borges. Following them, Burnham delivered an exceptionally strong speech in which he told the delegates that colonial Guyana (and ultimately the new independent state of Guyana) was not prepared to yield even a square inch of soil to Venezuela.

Further discussions continued on the following day with speeches made by the Foreign Ministers of both Great Britain and Venezuela who exchanged numerous suggestions for solving the controversy. Intense discussions took place on a draft agreement, which a team of British and Venezuelan officials, as well as Ramphal, had drawn up in the days preceding the conference, and by late afternoon, a consensus was reached. Shortly after, the British and Venezuelan Foreign Ministers, Michael Stewart and Ignacio Iribarren Borges, as well as Burnham, signed the document which became known as

The Geneva Agreement

The Agreement specified that a "Mixed Commission" of Guyanese and Venezuelan representatives would be established to seeking "satisfactory solutions for the practical settlement of the controversy between Venezuela and the United Kingdom which has arisen as the result of the Venezuelan contention that the Arbitral Award of 1899 about the frontier between British Guiana and Venezuela is null and void".

The Agreement also provided that "no new claim or enlargement of an existing claim to territorial sovereignty in these territories (of Venezuela and British Guiana) shall be asserted while this Agreement is in force, nor shall any claim whatsoever be asserted otherwise than in the Mixed Commission while that Commission is in being".

The British Government, as stipulated in the Agreement, would remain as a party to it even after Guyana achieved independence.

After Guyana's Independence on May 26, 1966 and the departure of all British Forces stationed in-country, Venezuela reasserted its claim to the disputed territory.

On October 12, 1966, Guyana discovered that Venezuelan military and civilian personnel had occupied the Guyanese half of Ankoko Island in the Cuyuni River. The Venezuelans had begun developing an airfield and mining facilities on the island. Prime Minister Burnham protested the occupation and demanded Venezuela's complete withdrawal and the removal of the facilities. Dismissing the protest, Venezuela countercharged that Ankoko Island had always been Venezuelan territory. With Guyana unable to force a Venezuelan withdrawal, Ankoko Island remained occupied.

The Ankoko Island incident was followed in July 1968 by Venezuela's extension of its territorial waters to twelve nautical miles off its coast including the disputed region. Because Guyana claimed only a three-nautical-mile limit, Venezuela's decree in effect established a claim over coastal waters from three to twelve nautical miles off Guyana's western coast. Guyana immediately condemned the Venezuelan decree, and Britain voiced its concern to the Venezuelan ambassador in London. Political sparring continued for six months until the incident was overshadowed by new events.

On January 4, 1969, Prime Minister Burnham reported that disturbances had occurred in the Rupununi region of southern Guyana. The historically independent-minded ranchers of the Rupununi's savannahs had unsuccessfully attempted a secessionist revolt. The police station in Lethem, the major government post in the region, had been attacked on January 2. Five (5) policemen and one civilian employee of the police had been killed. The insurgents then seized and blocked most area airstrips. The airstrip at Manari, 4.5 miles / 8 km from Lethem, was left open, apparently for the insurgents' own use. Responding quickly, the Guyanese government flew GDF forces to Manari. Surprised by the rapid government action, the insurgents fled to Venezuela and order was restored.

After the Defence Force put down the rebellion, the insurgents took refuge in Venezuelan border towns. Venezuela denied any wrongdoing and declared the insurgents Venezuelan citizens because they had inhabited land claimed by Venezuela. Guyana bitterly protested the Venezuelan actions.

Saturday, February 21 through Sunday, February 22, 1970 hours before Guyana became a Republic, the troubled peace along the border was again shattered when Venezuelan armed forces on occupied Ankoko Island, unprovoked, opened a furious barrage of small arms and mortar fire on the Guyana Defence Force (GDF) outpost at Eteringbang. Upon immediate instructions from Prime Minister Burnham, the men at the outpost were ordered not to return fire. The matter was promptly reported to the United Nations (UN) and on March 3, Venezuela closed the border.

Throughout the troubled period, the border commission had continued to meet. The commission's four-year term expired in early 1970 with the dispute unresolved. Nonetheless, on June 18, 1970, the governments of Venezuela, Britain, and Guyana signed the Protocol of Port-of-Spain. This protocol, which supplemented the 1899 agreement, placed a twelve-year moratorium on the border dispute. The protocol provided for continued discussions, a suspension of territorial claims, and automatic renewal of the protocol if it remained uncontested after the twelve years. In 1981 Venezuela announced that it would not renew the protocol.

1973 – The Upper Mazaruni River Hydro Electric - Project. Venezuela's deliberate attempt to hinder and deter the development of Guyana. For details, see text on The Upper Mazaruni River Hydro Electric Project.

September 2013 - Venezuela's Navy intercepted and arrested a seismic vessel and its crew that had been conducting tests in an offshore concession that Guyana granted to a Texas-headquartered company, Anadarko Petroleum Corporation.

May 20, 2015 - A decades-long search for oil offshore Guyana has finally yielded success with Exxon Mobil, an American Corporation headquartered in Irving, Texas, reporting a "significant oil discovery" in the 'Stabroek Block' located approximately 120 miles / 190 km offshore Guyana. On May 26, 2015 Venezuela's President Nicholas Maduro signed a decree that now claims an entire portion of Guyana's territory into the Atlantic Ocean that includes the Stabroek Block.

This recent decree without longitude and latitude lines claims all the territorial waters within the 200 mile range thus blocking Guyana's access to resources in that area of the Atlantic Ocean. Unlike the first decree issued by Venezuelan President Raul Leoni in July 1968 that purportedly claims sovereignty over a 12-mile strip of Guyana's continental shelf along the Essequibo Coast, this decree by Maduro takes in an oil-rich concession that Guyana has granted to US oil giant ExxonMobil.

It should be noted, prior to ExxonMobil's announcement on May 20, 2015 that it had found a "significant" oil deposit, Venezuela had twice written to the Guyanese subsidiary of that company warning it against continuing the search for oil because that maritime area and the entire Essequibo Region — the land area from Venezuela east to the Essequibo River — were part of its territory.

APPENDIX A

Guyanese, Chiefs of Staff

Brigadier General Clarence Price	1969 - 1979
Major General Norman McLean	1979 - 1990
Major General Joseph Singh	1990 - 2000
Major General Michael Atherly	2000 - 2004
Brigadier General Edward Collins	2004 - 2007
Rear Admiral Gary Best	2007 - 2013
Brigadier General Mark Phillips	2013 - Current

Brigadier Clarence Price 1969 - 1979

He was the first Guyanese Officer who became Chief of Staff of the Guyana Defence Force (GDF) in March 1969. He replaced Lieutenant Colonel Ronald James Pope, when he retired. Prior to his military career, he worked as a stenographer at the United States Air Force Base at Atkinson Field in 1943. Likewise, he worked in British Guiana Civil Service; as well as, enlisting in the South Caribbean Force (SCF). Additionally, he served in England with the Royal Air Force (RAF) during World War II. He was a Radar Operator and achieved the rank of Leading Aircraftman (LAC). It is a junior rank in some Air Forces, between Aircraftman and Senior Aircraftman; having a NATO Rank Code of OR-2. The rank badge is a horizontal two-bladed propeller; it originated in the Royal Air Force, when it was formed in 1918.

On his return to Guiana, he joined the British Guiana Volunteer Force (BGVF). When he was not on duty with the British Guiana Volunteer Force (BGVF); he worked at the Ministry of Home Affairs; in the title role of Assistant Secretary, responsible for defence matters. In 1951 he joined the Guyana Defence Force (GDF); afterwards, he was commissioned with rank of Second Lieutenant. In January 1966, he was posted to the GDF as a Major. In April 1969, he was elevated to the rank of Lt. Colonel and became the first Guyanese to be named Chief-of-Staff (COS) of the Defence Force, a position he held until his retirement in July 1979.

Medals:

Efficiency Decoration

Independence Medal

Military Service Star (MSS), the highest national award for distinguished military service

Major General Norman Gordon McLean 1979 - 1990

He was commissioned as a second Lieutenant in the British Guiana Volunteer Force in 1957 after having joined the BGVF as a private in 1954. He left the next year to become a cadet in the British Guiana Police Force (BGPF) as one of the first local cadet officers. During his service in the force he attended and successfully completed courses at the police college in the United Kingdom and the International Police Academy in Washington, USA and rose to the rank of Cadet Officer to that Assistant Commissioner.

Major General McLean was then seconded to the Guyana National service upon its formation as its first Director General in 1974. On July 12, 1979 he was promoted to the rank of Brigadier; and was posted to the Guyana Defence Force and appointed Chief of Staff and Coordinator of the Joint service. He was promoted to Major General in 1985. His academic qualifications include a Diploma in Public Administration and a Bachelor's degree in Public Management, both form the University of Guyana, and a Master's Degree in Security Management from the University of Leicester, UK. Major General McLean retired on December 1, 1990.

Medals, Badges, Awards

Colonial Police Medal for Meritorious Service

Independence Medal

Military Service Star (MSS), the highest national award for distinguished military service

Military Service Medal (MSM)

Major General Joseph Govinda Singh 1990 - 2000

He was among the first batch of Guyanese selected by the British Army in 1965 to attend officer cadet training in the UK, in preparation for the establishment of the Guyana Defence Force of independent Guyana. He is a graduate of Mons Officer Cadet School, Aldershot (1966); the School of Infantry, Warminster (1970); the Army School of Education, Beaconsfield (1970); the Army Staff College, Camberley (1977); and, the Royal College of Defence Studies, Belgrave Square, UK (1995).

His service as a commissioned officer spanned 34 years commencing as a Second Lieutenant on June 04 1966; Lieutenant 1968; Captain 1970; Major 1972; Lieutenant Colonel 1975; Colonel 1979; Brigadier 1986; and, Major General 1999.

In addition, he held the appointments of Officer Commanding Reconnaissance Platoon, Battalion Adjutant, and General Staff Officer Grade 2 and Grade 1, responsible for all Operations and Training in the Guyana Defence Force. From 1981 to 1990 he was seconded as Director General of the Guyana National Service.

He was re-assigned to the Guyana Defence Force as Chief of Staff in March 1990 until he retired in 2000. He is a graduate of the University of Guyana (Public Administration), the UK Royal College of Defence Studies (Post Graduate - International Relations and Strategic Studies), and of the School of Earth and Environmental Sciences, Greenwich University, UK (MSc in Tourism & Protected Landscape Management).

Medals, Badges, Awards:

Military Service Star (MSS) the highest national award for distinguished military service and five other national and military awards from Guyana, national awards from Brazil, Venezuela, Suriname, France and Cuba.

Major General Michael Atherly 2000 – 2004

Major General Michael Ulric Atherly was commissioned as a Second Lieutenant on May 20th 1971. He was promoted to Lieutenant 1974, Captain in 1976, Major in 1980, Lieutenant Colonel in 1987, Colonel in 1993, Brigadier in 2000 and Major General in May 2004. He held several appointments including: Officer Commanding Colonel Ulric Pilgrim Officer Cadet School; Commanding Officer 3 Special Forces Battalion; Commanding Officer, Training Corps; Commander 1 Infantry Battalion Group and Colonel General Staff, Defence Headquarters. Major General Atherly also served as Deputy Commander of a multi-national Commonwealth Military Training Team to Uganda.

He was appointed Chief of Staff in April 2000. He was educated at numerous international military institutions including the Canadian Staff School in Toronto, the Canadian Command and Staff College in Kingston Ontario, the Camberley Command and Staff College in the United Kingdom, the Lester Pearson Peacekeeping College in Nova Scotia Canada and the National Defence University in the United States of America.

Major General Atherly was admitted to the United States National Defence University International Fellows Hall of Fame (Washington DC) in October 2004. Major General Michael Atherly retired in April 2004.

Medals, Badges, Awards:

Military Service Medal (MSM)

Military Service Star (MSS), the highest national award for distinguished military service.

Brigadier General Edward Collins May 2004 – September 2007

He joined the Guyana Defence Force (GDF) as an Officer Cadet in 1973, and was commissioned as a Second Lieutenant on July 24, 1974. Brigadier General (retired) Collins has held a number of appointments in the GDF culminating with the Chief of Staff Guyana Defence Force. He retired on 26th September 2007. Brigadier General (retired) Collins has also served overseas as Commander of the CARICOM Contingent during the United Nations Mission in Haiti (UNMIH) from March to September 1995. Then, he became the first Caribbean Officer to command the CARICOM Forces on a United Nations Mission.

His military education and training includes the Company Commander Course -Peoples' Liberation Army, People's Republic of China; the GDF's Junior Staff Course, the Combat Team Commander Course - United Kingdom; the GDF's Military Law Course, the Canadian Forces Staff Course, Toronto, Canada; the Canadian Land Forces Command & Staff Course, Fort Frontenac, Kingston, Canada; the Civil Military Strategy for Internal Development -Special Operations School of Defence and Development US Air Force, Fort Walton Beach, Florida; the Command and General Staff Course - Fort Leavenworth, Kansas, USA; the Law of Armed Conflict – Canada; the Advance

Continental Defence Course - Inter-American Defence College, Fort Mc Leslie J. Nair, Washington D.C.

Brigadier General (retired) Collins is a graduate of the University of Guyana with a B.Soc. (Hons) in Public Management in 1996; and Central Michigan University, United States, he graduated in 1997 with a MSc in General Administration.

Medals, Awards

Military Service Medal (MSM)
Border Defence Medal
Military Efficiency Medal
Twenty-Fifth Anniversary Medal

Prime Minister's Medal for the Best Graduating Student in the Diploma of Public Management, University of Guyana.

On 3rd April, 2008, he was the first Guyanese to be inducted in the International Officers Hall of Fame at the Command and General Staff College, Fort Leavenworth Kansas, United States of America. The following week, on 9th April, he was inducted not only as the first from Guyana but also the English-speaking Caribbean into the Hall of Honour at the Inter American Defense College, Fort Leslie J. Me Nair, Washington, D.C. U.S.A. Other inductees of the latter College included the President of Chile, Madame Michele Bachelet, who was a student of the Class of XXXVII.

Rear Admiral Gary Best 2007 - 2013

The Rear Admiral was adjudged the best graduating student of the Standard Officers Course Number Nine (9) at the Colonel Pilgrim Officer Cadet School in 1981. He successfully completed his maritime training from 1981 to 1985 in the Brazilian Navy. He is fluent in Portuguese.

As Commander Coast Guard during the period of June 1994 to September 1999; he was responsible for the establishment of the Coast Guard Law Enforcement Districts throughout Guyana;

in addition to the development of a Maritime Information System Database. Rear Admiral Best was the Strategic and Long-Range Planner and Principal Staff Officer in the Force. His areas of expertise included Intelligence, Operations and Training. He served as the Colonel Administration and Quartering, and Special Duties Legal Officer.

With an ardent awareness of academic excellence, he attained a Bachelor's Degree in Law from the University of Guyana. He was admitted to the Guyana Bar in 2005. His qualifications include a Legal Education Certificate from the Hugh Wooding Law School in Trinidad and Tobago, and a Master of Science Degree in International Relations from the University of the West Indies (UWI) in 2011. He is studying for a PhD in International Relations at the UWI in the research category of Climate Change Financing.

Medals, Badges, Awards:

Military Service Star (MSS) the highest national award for distinguished military service. He received the Admiral Tamandare Merit Medal from Brazil and the Medal of Carobobo from Venezuela.

Brigadier General Mark Phillips 2013 - Current.

He joined the Guyana Defence Force (GDF) as an Officer Cadet. On August 7, 1981, he attended the Standard Military Course #26, Royal Military Academy, Sandhurst, UK. On February 17, 1982 he was commissioned as a Second Lieutenant and was subsequently promoted to Lieutenant (1985); Captain (1989); Major (1994); Lieutenant Colonel (2001); Colonel (2007) and Brigadier / Chief of Staff on August 19, 2013.

His appointments include – Platoon Commander II Infantry Battalion (1982-83); Troop Commander 33 Jungle Company/ Special Forces Battalion (1983-84) ; Principal Instructor Colonel Ulric Pilgrim Officer Cadet School (1984) ; Officer Commanding 'C' Company, 1st Infantry Battalion (1988) ; General Staff

Officer (GSO) 1,2, and 3 (1993-2000) ; Base Commander Camp Stephenson ((2002); General Staff Officer 1 (2006); Colonel Administration & Quartering (2006); Colonel General Staff (2008) ; Inspector General (2011); Guyana's Delegate to Inter-American Defense Board (2008) ; Guyana's Non Resident Military Attaché to Venezuela (2010).

His military education and training includes: Internal Security Studies (1983); Basic Paratrooper and Parachute Jump Master training in Brazil (Aug 10 – Sept 25,1984) ; Junior Command and Staff Course (1985); Senior Command and Staff Course (1990); Airport Crisis Management International Civil Aviation Organization, Mexico (1994); Disaster Management, University of the West-Indies, Trinidad & Tobago (1996);Human Rights in Modern Peacekeeping, Canada (1997); Defense Planning and Resources Management, USA (2003); Command and General Staff Officers' Course, Fort Leavenworth, Kansas, USA (2005); Canadian Security Studies Programme, Canada (2008); Advance Defense and Security Studies Programme – Inter American Defense College, USA (2011).

Brigadier General Phillips holds a Bachelor's Degree in Public Management from the University of Guyana (1998), and a Master's Degree in Public Sector Management from La Pontificia Universidad Catolica Madre y Maestra in the Dominican Republic (2000).

Medals, Badges, Awards:

Parachute/Master Parachutist Badge (Jump Master)

25th Anniversary Commemoration Medal

40th Anniversary Commemoration Medal,

Border Defence Medal,

Military Efficiency Medal,

Military Service Medal (MSM),

Military Service Star (MSS) the highest national award for distinguished military service.

He also received the Admiral Tamandare Merit Medal from Brazil, the Peace Keeper Medal from Brazil, and the Star of Carobobo Medal from Venezuela.

APPENDIX B

Guyana Defence Force Commanders

Colonel Ulric Pilgrim	January 1972 – July 1978
Colonel Leonard B. Muss	July 1978 – September 1978
Colonel Carl B. Morgan	September 1978 – July 1979
Brigadier General David A. Granger	July 1979 – December 1990

Colonel Ulric Pilgrim January 1972 - July 1978

Ulric Pilgrim is a former Commander of the Guyana Defence Force. His military service started in 1956 when he enlisted in the BGVF as a private soldier. In that year, too, he joined the British Guiana Civil Service and served for several years in the Treasury Department.

He reached the rank of Corporal in 1964 and commissioned as a Second Lieutenant. In his last eight months of service, he was embodied on full-time service, mainly on the West Coast Demerara during the disturbances of 1964-1965.

When the British Guiana Special Service Unit (BGSSU) was established, he was in the first batch three officer cadets recruited. Shortly after, three more officer cadets were recruited. There six recruits, were then sent to Mons Officer Cadet School in the UK in 1965. He returned to serve in the BGSSU, which, at that time, was under the administration of the British Guyana Police Force (BGPF) and the watchful eye of the British Garrison Commander; as a cadet officer.

On the approach of Independence, members of the BGSSU, were given the option of remaining in the BGPF or joining the proposed national army, to be called the Guyana Defence Force (GDF). He opted for the GDF and was soon appointed Adjutant to the Chief of Staff, Lieutenant Colonel Ronald Pope, the leader of the UK Army's Staffing Administration Training Team (SATT).

Ulric Pilgrim was promoted to the rank of Lieutenant and then Captain in this staff position. Other appointments he held were; Officer Commanding 'C' Company; Training Wing; General Staff Officer 2 in the rank of Major; and, finally, Force Commander in the rank of a Colonel (1972-1979).

During his tenure as Commander, he oversaw evolution of the GDF as a Force devoted not only to territorial defence but also economic development. There were significant improvements in the agriculture, engineer construction and fishing. The Force also increased its manpower strength and acquired ships, aircraft and other equipment to enable it counter threats to the country's territorial integrity.

He attended various training courses including; the Commonwealth Jungle Warfare School, Malaysia (1968); Junior Division Staff College, Warminister, UK, 1970; Army School of Education, Beaconsfield, UK 1970; Army Staff College, Camberly,(UK), (1971); as well as Royal College of Defence Studies, (UK) (1978). He also led military delegations to Cuba, Yugoslavia, Somalia and the USA.

Colonel Ulric Pilgrim was awarded the Military Service Medal MSM. In 1980, the Officer Cadet School was named the Colonel Ulric Pilgrim Officer Cadet School (CUPOCS) in his honour.

Medals:

Independence Medal

Military Service Medal - MSM

Military Efficiency Medal

Colonel Leonard B. Muss July 1978 – September 1978

He started his uniformed service in the Queens College Cadet Corps (QCCC). In 1955 he was Commissioned as a Second Lieutenant in the British Guiana Volunteer Force (BGVF) and subsequently promoted to Lieutenant. In January 1966, he entered the Guyana Defence Force with the rank of Captain and in May 1966, he joined the 1st Battalion as second-in-command of 'A' Company.

On January 5, 1968, he led '1' Company (formerly A) into the interior/hinterlands at Bartica; thus making the first Rifle Company to be billeted in the interior. His professional military education, include several training courses at foreign military institutions such as the Commonwealth Jungle Warfare School in Johore Bahru, Malaysia ; Company Commanders Course-School of Infantry, Warminster, UK.

On January 1, 1972, he was promoted to Lieutenant Colonel and appointed Commanding Officer of the 2nd Battalion. In January 1973, he remained as Commanding Officer upon the name change of the 2nd Battalion to Border Operations Command. In 1975, he was named Brigade Commander of the newly formed Infantry Brigade; upon the merging of the Internal Operations Command and Border Operations Command.

In July 1978, he was promoted to Colonel and appointed Commander of the GDF.

In Sept 1978, he resigned.

Medals:

Efficiency Decoration

Independence Medal

Border Defence medal

Colonel Carl B. Morgan September 1978 – July 1979

He started his uniformed services when he joined the Queen's College Cadet Corp (QCCC) where he rose to the rank of Cadet Officer, a feat achieved by few while still students.

A few months after leaving school in July 1964, he was selected as one of the first six cadet officers of the British Guiana Special Service Unit (BGSSU) and attended Mons Officer Cadet School in the UK in February 1965. On his return, he was commissioned on July 9, 1965 and appointed a platoon commander. He opted to transfer to the newly formed Guyana Defense Force (GDF) when it was formed on 1 November 1965.

In 1966, when the British Garrison was withdrawing from British Guiana, Carl Morgan toured the North-West borders (Regions 1) as Intelligence Officer as part of his takeover from the Garrison GSO3 (Int), becoming the first GDF officer to visit the border markers in the North West. In October 1966, he was aboard the first aircraft to land at Eteringbang at the start of the Ankoko Island crisis.

Post 1966, Morgan served in numerous appointments including Intelligence Officer / Signals Officer. In 1967, he was appointed the first platoon commander of the newly formed Reconnaissance (Recce) Platoon. Also, in 1967 he was appointed Adjutant of the 1st Battalion.

Between the period 1968-1970, he was Company Commander 5 Company, 2nd Battalion where he attended the Jungle Warfare – Commonwealth Jungle Warfare School in Malaysia (1969) ; Company Commanders Course- School of Infantry, Warminster,

UK and Methods of Instruction – Army School of Instructional Technology, Beconsfield, UK both in 1970.

1971 - Morgan became Officer Commanding the Army's Training Corps. Shortly thereafter, he became the Second in Command of the 1st Battalion before leaving to take Command of 'Internal Operations Command', a position he held between1972-1974.

1975 – Morgan attended the Army Staff College, Camberley, UK and held the title of General Staff Officer Grade 1 (GSO 1 Co-ord); by 1978 he was Commander of the 1st Infantry Brigade and also acted as Force Commander (1978) before returning to his prior position as Brigade Commander.

1979 – 1981 - Morgan was seconded and appointed, Chief Administrative Officer at Matthews Ridge/Arakaka/ Port Kaituma (MATARKAI) Development Authority and Regional Commander Guyana Peoples Militia – Region 1.

1981-1982- Morgan was attached to GUYSTAC as Operations Director, Guyana Fisheries Limited. Thereafter he returned to the Force to assume the appointment of Commandant Guyana Peoples' Militia (GPM) (1982 -1990).

In 1987, he attended the National Defence College in New-Delhi, India where he earned his Master's degree in Defence Studies. In 1988, he was appointed Commander Operations and Training of the GDF while still holding the appointment of Commandant of GPM.

In 1990, Morgan retired from military service upon his appointment as Guyana Ambassador to Suriname, a position he held through 1992.

Through his studies, Morgan also holds the Diploma in Public Administration from the University of Guyana.

Medals, Badges, Awards:

Independence Medal

Military Efficiency Medal

Military Service Medal,

30th Anniversary Medal of the Cuban Armed Forces,

Carabobo Star of Venezuela – 1st Class,

Military Service Star, 25th Anniversary Commemorative Medal of the Guyana Defence Force

Grand Ribbon of the Honorary Order of the Palm - Suriname.

Brigadier General David A. Granger July 1979 – December 1990

He was a member of the Queen's College Cadet Corps (QCCC), he joined the GDF as an officer cadet in 1965 and was commissioned as a second Lieutenant in 1966 upon his return from Mons Officer Cadet School in Aldershot, England and assigned as a platoon commander to the newly formed 'C Rifle Company' of the 1st Battalion.

He received his professional military training at the Army Command and Staff College in Nigeria; the Jungle Warfare Instruction Centre in Brazil; and the School of Infantry, respectively, in the United Kingdom.

During his military service, he held a variety of appointments including planning officer for the establishment of the Guyana National Service (1973-74) and the Guyana People's Militia (1976-1977). He also led military delegations to Brazil, Cuba, Germany, Guinea, Korea, Somalia and Yugoslavia.

He graduated with the Master of Social Science Degree in Political Science, and the Bachelor of Arts Degree in History, from the University of Guyana; and the post-graduate diploma in International Relations from the University of the West Indies. He was also an Internal Fellow on the Defence Planning and Resource Management Seminar at the Center for Hemispheric Defence Studies of the National Defence University and attended the Counterterrorism Educators' Workshop at the Joint Special Operations University, Florida, USA.

He has presented several papers on defence and security topics to international and national academic conferences including: "Civil Violence, Domestic Terrorism and Internal Security in Guyana, 1953-2003"; Convention and Convenience: A Preliminary Study of Women Soldiers in the Anglophone Caribbean with Special Reference to the Women's Army Corps of the Guyana Defence Force, 1967-2002"; and, Defence and Diplomacy in the Subordinate System: The Experience of Guyana".

David Granger is a former member of the Disciplined Forces Commission; Co-Chairman of the Border and National Security Committee; Member of the National Security Strategy Planning Committee; Chairman of the Central Intelligence Committee; Member of the National Drug Law Enforcement Committee; and Member of the Guyana Defence Board.

He was appointed Commander of the Guyana Defence Force in 1979; he was promoted to the rank of Brigadier General. He was appointed as National Security Advisor to the late President Desmond Hoyte in 1990 and retired from the GDF in 1992.

Medals, Badges, Awards:

Military Service Star, the highest national award for distinguished military service

Military Service Medal

Military Efficiency Medal

Border Defence Medal and other service awards

APPENDIX C

Brigadier General Jullian (Bruce) Lovell - First resident Military Attaché to Brazil - Appendix C

On October 20, 1978 he entered the Guyana Defence Force as a Private before entering the Officer Cadet Course # 8 in 1979. After successfully completing his officer training, he was commissioned as a Second Lieutenant on February 20, 1980 and assigned to the Training Corps as Principal Instructor. Thereafter, he entered the 13 Guards Battalion as a Platoon Commander.

On July 1, 1982, he was promoted to Lieutenant and between 1982 -1983; he was the Principal Instructor at the Colonel Ulric Pilgrim Officer Cadet School. In 1984, he attended the Junior Command and Staff Course at Colonel Cecil Martindale Command and Staff School, Guyana. He was adjudged runner-up, Best Graduating Student. He was also Adjutant, 13 Guards Battalion. 1985 – 1988, he was Aide de Camp to President Hugh Desmond Hoyte. On January 1, 1986, he was promoted to Captain.

In 1990, he was Staff Officer Grade (2), Administration; Officer Commanding A Company, 1 Infantry Battalion. In 1992, he attended the Senior Command and Staff Course, Colonel Cecil Martindale Command and Staff School, Guyana where he was adjudged the Best Graduating Student; Best Oral Presentation; Best Service Paper.

In 1993, he attended the Civil and Military Strategy for Internal Development, United States Air Force Special Operations School, Hurlburt Field, Okaloosa County, Florida, USA. Also, between, 1993 - 1994, he was Officer Commanding, Public Relations and Education Department. On January 1, 1994, he was promoted to Major. Between, 1994 – 1997, he was Staff Officer Grade One (1), Operations and Training.

In 1996, he attended the Peacekeeping Management, Command and Staff Course, Lester B. Pearson, Canadian International Peacekeeping Training Centre, Canada. Between, 1997 – 1998, he was Base Commander, Base Camp Ayanganna. Also, in 1998, he attended the Public Affairs Officer Course, Defence Information School, Maryland, USA1998 - 1999; he was Officer Commanding, Colonel Cecil Martindale Command and Staff School. In 1999 he was Commanding Officer, CARICOM Battalion, Field Training Exercise, Guyana. 1999 – 2001, he was Second in Command, First Infantry Battalion Group. On July 1, 2000, he was promoted to Lieutenant Colonel. Also in 2000, he was Commanding Officer, CARICOM Battalion, Command Post Exercise.

Medals:

Military Service Medal (MSM)

Military Efficiency Medal

25th Anniversary Medal

40th Anniversary Medal

Silver Medal of National Defence (France)

Peacemaker Medal (Brazil)

Inter- American Defence Board Medal

APPENDIX D

Colonel Cecil E. Martindale, First Commandant, Guyana People's Militia

He had a successful career in the Public Service, before he was seconded as a Major to the newly formed Guyana Defence Force (GDF) on March 7, 1966. During his military career he attained the rank of Colonel, with a distinguished record of service to the Military Forces.

His military career started in 1948 when he enlisted in the ranks of the British Guiana Volunteer Force (BGVF). Three years later in August 1951, he was commissioned in the rank of Second Lieutenant, promoted to Lieutenant a year later and he became a Captain in November 1955. In 1958, he was the Force Adjutant and on May 1, he participated in the presentation of the Queen's Colour in Georgetown during the visit of Her Royal Highness, Princess Margaret.

In February 1961 he was promoted to Major, Lieutenant Colonel in May 1967 and Colonel in May 1976. In the BGVF, his duties ranged from Platoon Commander in 1951 to company Commander in July 1960. In March 1966, Major Martindale was appointed Officer Commanding (OC) of Head Quarters (HQ) Company 1st Battalion of the GDF following his secondment from the Public Service and in June 1966, he became Staff Officer at HQ 1st Battalion. In January 1968, he was appointed Commanding Officer 2nd Battalion. In July 1969, he was Chief of Staff (Acting).

In December 1971, he was recalled to the Public Service but returned when he was appointed Commandant Guyana People's Militia in May 1976. On February 28, 1981, Colonel Martindale attained the compulsory retirement age, but he was retained the next day, March 1, 1981, to his final retirement on July 1, 1989. On his retirement, he held the appointment of Principal Staff Office in the Defence Headquarters.

As of this writing, Colonel Martindale is the longest living member of the BGVF, and one of the stalwarts of the Military service in Guyana. He contributed immensely to the development of the Reserves and was the first Commandant of the People's Militia from its formation in 1976. He was deeply interested in sports, band music and promoted the early development of Hockey and the playing of steel band music in the Force. He held a variety of appointments both in Command and Staff in the Army and Guyana People's Militia. He has over nearly forty years of Militia Service and has greatly enriched the life of the Defence Forces; with his well-known wit and profound professional spirit.

Upon discharge, Colonel Martindale was noted as an outstanding Officer, leader, and gentleman, who was well respected by all his subordinates and functional superiors. He was accorded national honours for his exemplary service and in 1987 the Staff School was renamed in his honour, "Colonel Cecil Martindale Command and Staff School"

Medals, Badges, Awards:

Efficiency Decoration

Independence Medal

Border Defence Medal

Military Service Medal

Military Service Star, the highest national award for distinguished military service

Military Efficiency Medal

APPENDIX E

Colonel Desmond Roberts - First Officer selected to raise the National Flag
The Golden Arrowhead on
Independence Day – May 26, 1966

In 1954, he joined the Queens College Cadet Corps (QCCC). He was one of the first six officers of the British Guiana Special Service Unit (BGSSU); to be selected for training at Mons officer cadet school, UK in 1965. On his return he chose the option of joining the newly formed GDF in November 1965.

He was bestowed the distinguished honour, of raising the Golden Arrowhead, the Nation's flag in the National Park on Independence night on 25-26 May 1966. Later that year, he led his platoon to the border, after Guyana's half of Ankoko Island, had been occupied by the Venezuelan National Armed Forces (FAN).

In 1967, he gained much experience as a staff to the Chief of Staff, Colonel Ronald Pope, before being appointed Officer Commanding (OC) No. 4 Company in 1968. In early 1969, he commanded a company in the Rupununi Operation, to quell the rebellion started by cattle ranchers. He was appointed

General Staff Officer 2 (1970-71); and Second in Command, 2nd Battalion in 1972.

In May 1973, he was promoted to the rank of Major and sent as the first Military Director of the Guyana Youth Corps (GYC) and Assistant Director General of the Guyana National Service (GNS) in 1974; Deputy Director General in 1976; and Director General 1979-81. As Director General, he was instrumental in launching the International Association of National Service Organization (IANSO) in Lusaka, (1980).

He was appointed Military Attaché to Brazil (1982-1984) but functioned out of the Defence Secretariat. In 1984, he was given the responsibility of coordinating the North Korean, Guyanese and UNEP consultant terms constructing the small Eclipse Falls Hydro-Power project and, in 1986, he served as Commander, Administration and Logistic, until 1990, when he retired. He organized the first GDF Athletic Sports, in 1967, and served as President of the Amateur Athletic Association of Guyana (1976-1979 and 1986-1989), managing a team to the Seoul Olympics (1988); President of the Masters Athletic Association (1982-1989); and Vice-President of the Guyana Badminton Association.

He took the Advanced Infantry Commander (UK) and Army Command and Staff Course (Nigeria). He received his degree in Finance, along with several awards, from the University of Maryland, in 1993, and the Master of Urban Planning and Management degree at the New School University in Manhattan.

Medals:

Independence Medal

Border Defence Medal

Military Service Medal

Military Efficiency Medal

APPENDIX F

Colonel Harry Basil Hinds, First Commander of Maritime Corps

Harry Basil Hinds entered the GDF as an officer cadet in 1966, attended Mons Officer Cadet School (MOCS) in the UK in March 1966. While at MOCS, he won the appointment of Under Officer (UO) in Salerno Company which meant that he held the position as the most senior cadet at the Commonwealth officer's training establishment in the UK. That was only the first of many firsts

He was the first officer to attend the Mortar Officers' course at the School of Infantry, UK (1967). Upon his return, he established the GDF's mortar platoon which played a crucial role in 'Operation Climax,' launched on Tuesday, August 19, 1969.

He was the first GDF officer to qualify as a parachutist at Abingdon, UK (1968); the first officer to attend the Support Company Commanders' Course at Netheravon, UK (1970); and was only the Second GDF officer to attend the Junior Command and Staff Course at Warminster, UK (1971). As a result of this qualification, he was able to join the Training Corps to conduct the first formal junior and senior staff courses.

He was later to attend the Army Staff Course at Camberly, UK (1984) and the Civil-Military Strategy for Internal Development Course in Florida, USA (1995).

Harry Hinds was the founder, and the first Commanding Officer, of the GDF Coast Guard. Although trained as a ground force officer, in 1967, while attached to the Training Wing at Atkinson Field now Camp Stephenson, he became involved in the administration of the small Marine Wing that was assembled at Thomas Lands now Camp Ayanganna where the Force's few sailors then lived.

His greatest contribution to the Force and the country was to transform the Marine wing into an effective Coast Guard. In the heyday of the Coast Guard, daily newspapers never tired of telling of the arrests and seizures of foreign unlicensed fishing vessels. These achievements were the result of careful planning and forceful execution under Harry Hinds' command.

He was also the first military commissioner of the Civil Defence Commission (CDC). He helped to design systems for the Commission and chaired the committee which was engaged in negotiating the World Bank loan for the Guyana El Nino Emergency Assistance Project.

He wrote and published three articles on maritime security in the Guyana Review: The Coast Guard's Challenge; Fishing in Troubled Waters; and, Food, Fuel and Force.

Harry Hinds retired in 2000 and died in January 2003.

Medals, Badges:

Parachute Badge

Military Service Medal (MSM)

Military Efficiency Medal

Border Defence Medal

Commemoration Medal

APPENDIX G

Colonel Fairbairn E. Liverpool and 2nd Lieutenant Haydock West
First two Officer Cadets sent to the Royal Military, Academy, Sandhurst, UK

Col. Fairbairn Liverpool - Officer Cadet sent to the Royal Military Academy, Sandhurst, UK.

Colonel Fairbairn Egerton Liverpool is a former Adjutant General of the Guyana Defence Force. He joined the GDF as an officer cadet on December 29, 1965. He retired from the GDF on 31st December 2000, thirty-five years later. He was one of the first two officers to be trained at the Royal Military Academy (RMA), Sandhurst, in the UK (1966-1967).

During his service, he was appointed a Platoon Commander in No 4 Company, 2nd Battalion, and was assigned the responsibility for training. Also he served in several hinterland locations. In 1969 he was appointed Adjutant 1st Battalion and participated in Operation Climax in the New River. Over the next sixteen years, he was promoted, progressively and achieved the rank of Lieutenant Colonel in 1977, when he served as the General Staff Officer (GSO1 Coord). He also held the appointments of Officer Commanding No 4 Company; Commanding Officer Training

Corps and Air Corps; Commander of the Infantry Brigade; and Adjutant General.

In the field of sport he played a role in developing the GDF basketball team and participated in the competitions. Like several of his peers, he also lent his leadership and administrative skills at the national level in the administration of the Guyana Basketball Association.

He attended several military and academic training programmes; including the Commonwealth Jungle Warfare School in Malaya; the Infantry Commander's Course at the School of Infantry, Warminster (UK); the Army School of instruction Technology, Beaconsfield (UK); and the Brazilian Army Command and Staff School (ECEME). His academic qualifications include a Bachelor of Social Science degree (Management), University of Guyana, and a Master's degree in Development Administration from the University of Carleton, Canada.

In 1986, he was seconded to the Ministry of Home Affairs as the Permanent Secretary. He was the architect of Guyana's counter-narcotics strategy following Guyana's accession to the UN 1988 Convention, on Illicit Traffic in Narcotic Drugs and Psychotropic Substances. He was pivotal to the coordination of the fight against narcotics-trafficking. In 1998, he was seconded to become Coordinator of the Regional Coordinating Mechanism for Drugs, and Crime Control Programmes within the CARICOM Secretariat.

In December 2000, he officially reverted to the GDF and subsequently retired.

Medals:

Independence Medal

Jaguar Medal

Military Service Medal

Military Efficiency Medal

APPENDIX - H

Colonel Windee Algernon – First female promoted to Colonel in Guyana and the Caribbean

Ms. Windee Algernon entered the Guyana Defence Force on July 7, 1982 as an Ensign.

On August 25, 1982 she attended the Standard Officers Course and on December 25, 1982 upon successfully completing the course was promoted to the rank of 2nd Lieutenant. In April 1983 she was appointed Training Officer in the Training Corps, and in April 1985 was appointed a Staff Officer AG's Branch at Force Headquarters. In 1987 she was promoted to Lieutenant. Also on July 13, 1987 she attended the Junior Command Staff Course.

On January 1, 1991 she was promoted to a Captain (acting) and confirmed as Captain on January 1, 1992. On September 19, 1995 she completed the International Intelligence Officers Basic Course in the USA. January 1, 1998 she was promoted to Major (acting). She completed the International Intelligence Officers Advance course in the USA on July 29, and the Senior Command and Staff Course on Dec 18, 1998.

On January 1, 1999 she was promoted to Major, and on November 23, 2001 she completed the Regional Studies course in the USA. On August 17, 2002 she completed the Free & Equal Human Rights in Modern Peacekeeping Course in Canada. January 1, 2003 she was promoted to Lieutenant Colonel (acting), and on July 11, 2003 completed the International Intelligence Director course in the UK.

On January 1, 2004 she was promoted to Lieutenant Colonel.

On January 1, 2012 she was promoted to Colonel becoming the first female promoted to Colonel in Guyana and the Caribbean.

Medals:

Military Efficiency Medal

25th Anniversary Medal

40th Anniversary Medal

APPENDIX I

Regimental and Force Sergeant Major's (RSM/FSM)

The first Regimental Sergeant Major (RSM) of the Guyana Defence Force was Ronald Sergeant, a British citizen.

Subsequent to his departure in 1967, he was replaced by Claude McKenzie who became RSM of the 1st Battalion, and Eric Primo, RSM of the 2nd Battalion.

The role of RSM continued through December 31, 1980 when it was replaced by Force Sergeant Major (FSM).

The Warrant Officer's (WO) 1 appointed FSM effective January 1, 1981 to current period are:

WO 1 Sutton, Ulric - Jan 1, 1981 - Nov 03, 1982

WO 1 Beaton, Carlos - Nov 4, 1982 - Aug 31, 1985

WO 1 Austin, Wilfred - Sept 1, 1985 - July 13, 1989

WO 1 Nedd, Orville - Aug 9, 1989 - Dec 31, 1994

WO 1 Younge - Jan 1, 1995 - July 11, 1999

WO 1 George, A - July 12, 1999 - Sept 02, 2001

WO 1 Burnett, I - Sept 03, 2001 - Oct 19, 2001

WO 1 Simon, E - Oct 20, 2001 - Oct 21, 2002

WO 1 Semple, C - Oct 22, 2003 - Feb 05, 2006

WO 1 Hardy, L - Feb 18, 2006 - Oct 29, 2007

WO 1 Thomas, D S. - Oct 30, 2007 - Jan 29, 2013

WO 1 Marks, R - Jan 30, 2013 - Jan 26, 2014

WO 1 Richmond, W - Jan 27, 2014

WO 1 Holligan - May 14, 2014

APPENDIX J

Governors and British Troops stationed in British Guiana (1947 to 1966)

Governors and British Army Regiments in British Guiana 1953-1966

British Governors:

Sir Gordon James Lethem,	November 7, 1941	April 12, 1947
Sir Charles Campbell Woolley	April 12,1947	April 14,1953.
Sir Alfred William Savage	April 14,1953	October 25,1955.
Sir Patrick Muir Renison	October 25, 1955	December 22, 1958
Sir Ralph Francis Grey	December 22, 1958	March 7, 1964
Sir Richard Edmonds Luyt	March 7, 1964	May 26, 1966

Note: Lethem in the Rupununi was named after Governor Sir Gordon James Lethem

British Regiments:

For 13 years between October 1953 and October 1966, eighteen (18) British Regiments were stationed in British Guiana.

1) October 8, 1953 - 1st Battalion, Royal Welsh Fusiliers arrived from their British West Indies (BWI) base in Kingston, Jamaica

   (Up Park Camp), and British Honduras aboard two (2) Frigates, HMS BIGBURY BAY and

   HMS BurgHead with 100 men and 10 tons of store/ equipment, each, and the Cruiser HMS

   SUPERB with 500 men. After 2 weeks, the Regiment was replaced.

2) October 1953 - 1st Battalion, Argyll and Sutherland Highlanders.

3) October 1954 2nd Battalion, Royal Highland Regiment (Black Watch).

4) March 1956 - 1st Battalion Duke of Cornwall's Light Infantry. ## (sent from Bermuda).

5) March 1957- 1960: 1st Battalion Worcestershire Regiment (Arrived in Jamaica for their 3 year tour of duty in the Caribbean Region). A small contingent (Company size) was stationed in British Guiana. And on January 23, 1960 a joint ceremonial parade was held to celebrate their alliance with the British Guiana Volunteer Force (BGVF).

6) February 1960 -1963 - 1st Battalion, Royal Hampshire Regiment - (An advance party of a Rifle Company arrived in Jamaica for a 3 year tour of duty, replacing a Battalion of Worcestershire Regiment in March. The Royal Hampshire Regiment had 5 Companies including their HQ in the Caribbean Region - 2 in Jamaica, 1 in

British Honduras, 1 in British Guiana, and the fifth.was split between Nassau Bahamas and Bermuda).

7) January 1962 1st Battalion East Anglian (Royal Norfolk & Suffolk) Regiment

8) 1962 1st Battalion, Duke of Edinburgh's Royal Regiment

9) October 1962 1st Battalion Coldstream Guards - relieved #7

10) July 1963 1st & 2nd Battalion Green Jackets.

11) 1964 2nd Battalion Grenadier Guards.

12) March 1964 1st Battalion, Queens Own Buffs, The Royal Kent Regiment

13) May 1964 1st Battalion, Devonshire & Dorset Regiment -Departed Jan 1965

14) December 7, 1964 1st Battalion, King's Own Border Regiment

15) January 1965 1st Battalion, King's Manchester & Liverpool Regiment.

16) January 1965 1st Battalion, Lancashire Fusiliers -Departed October 1965

17) February 1965 3rd Parachute Regiment - Departed Feb 1966

18) M arch 1966 1st BN Middlesex Regiment, Duke of Cambridge Own-Departed 10/'66

About the Author

Lieutenant Colonel Compton Hartley Liverpool (Ret)

Lieutenant Colonel Compton Hartley Liverpool (Ret) began his Military Career in 1955 in the British Guiana Volunteer Force (BGVF) as a Private.

On November 1, 1965, he transitioned into the newly formed Guyana Defence Force (GDF) as a Corporal. Thereafter, he rose to the rank of Lt. Colonel on soldierly abilities alone, learning each day.

He served as Platoon, Company, Battalion, Base and Garrison Commander.

As of this writing, he is the first and only Soldier in the Guyana Defence Force to be awarded a Medal for Valour.

In 1990, he retired under the mandatory age of 55 after 25 years of active service in the Guyana Defence Force.

His memoir is very informative and details all major operations of the force.

About the Coauthor

Khalilah Megan Campbell

The 'Foundation of the Guyana Defence Force' by Lt. Colonel Compton Hartley Liverpool (Ret) has chronicled the origins of what will unfold to establish the military legacy of Guyana. This seminal and monumental publication will forever be indebted to Ms. Khalilah Megan Campbell, the coauthor, who has been an invaluable and indispensable asset in charting the completion of the book. She has worked tirelessly and assiduously in every facet of the manuscript to enrich the publication of this historic masterpiece.

This success has all been possible because of the unique and remarkable skills that Ms. Campbell possesses. She is an accomplished Guyanese, and her early exposure to national allegiance and eventually the military renders her adequately qualified to function in the pivotal role of guiding this publication through its meticulous formative stages.

Ms. Campbell's professional career has included responsibilities as a 'Conflict Resolution Mediator', 'Special Education Mediator', and a 'Writer'. More appropriately, her service in the Canadian Armed Forces – 735 (Winnipeg) Communication Regiment and the Guyana National Service (Finance Department) contributed direct relevance to her intuitive understanding of the 'Foundation of the Guyana Defence Force'.

Author's note

This military account presents two problems to a writer striving for the truth. First of all, a life condition free of memory lapses and impediments to accurately chronicle events, and the presence of an audience willing and eager to travel through the years down the path of historical events in order to relive and assess the sacrifices and heroics of an armed forces that made our nation great.

Honesty and accuracy were my objectives to the best of my ability and knowledge, for which if it were deemed necessary, I apologize for any inadvertent errors or omissions on my part.

Printed in the United States
By Bookmasters